GEORGE LUCAS COMPANION

HOWARD MAXFORD

B.T. Batsford • London

Printed by Polestar Wheatons Ltd, Exeter

For the Publishers

B.T. Batsford Ltd

583 Fulham Road

London SW6 5BY

ISBN 0 7134 8425 X

Acknowledgements

The author and publisher would like to thank Joel Finler for his co-operation and help with picture research for this book. Film stills are copyright to relevant Production Companies unless otherwise stated. Credits are due to: Hammer Films for pages 45 and 60; The Ladd Company for page 104, The M Company for page 123; Marvel Comics Group for page 126; Albert Ortega for pages 50, 108, 144, 150, 151, 154; Sue Schneider for pages 10, 37, 43, 55, 64, 68, 81, 92, 112; Tri-Star Pictures Inc for page 84; Twentieth Century Fox for page 13; Universal City Studios for page 73.

Thanks are also due to Gary Kurtz for generously giving his time and sharing his knowledge of George Lucas's work during the preparation of this book for publication.

Dedication

For my brother Heath, with whom I first saw Star Wars *way back when;*
For Ann Sweeney (and Brooper, too) who is mental about Star Wars
(actually she's just mental);
And for the great man himself, George Lucas, without whom the cinema
would have been a less exciting place.

CONTENTS

1

Back to the Future

For those who first saw *Star Wars* on its initial monumental release back in 1977, the year 1997 proved to be a curious one. To celebrate the movie's twentieth anniversary (and also to act as an appetite-whetting curtain-raiser to the first of three prequels then in pre-production), George Lucas re-released *Star Wars* (and its two sequels, *The Empire Strikes Back* and *The Return of the Jedi*) in a Special Edition format. In a clever marketing ploy, Lucas not only overhauled the film's sound and picture quality, but also added several new sequences. He also improved upon the effects. To no one's surprise, *Star Wars*, regarded by many as one of the all-time greats, again broke box office records. Not bad for a film two decades old and familiar through video and countless television airings.

   For those only used to seeing the film on the small screen, the theatrical re-release proved to be a revelation. For those who could recall that first release, it was like travelling back in time. The hype, the media blitz, the merchandising and the queues round the block. Back in 1977, *Star Wars* had redefined the blockbuster, ushering in not only a new style of filmmaking, but also the manner in which 'event' pictures were marketed. Twenty years on, *Star Wars* was using these self same techniques - now an industry staple - to bring in the

punters yet again. The public's appetite was, it seemed, insatiable as far as *Star Wars* was concerned.

And what of the man behind the *Star Wars* empire, George Lucas? One of the most astute operators in the modern motion picture business, he has subsequently become one of its wealthiest, thanks not only to the *Star Wars* movies, but also the *Indiana Jones* adventures. A brilliant businessman as well as a talented filmmaker, he has rarely put a foot wrong (though when he has done, he's done it big time, as with the atrocious *Howard the Duck*!). Yet for such an industry big hitter, Lucas is pretty much a private person. His public and media appearances are rare. Lucas prefers to let his work speak for him.

So what of Lucas's own story? How did he get to be the movie giant he is today? How did he earn his vaunted reputation and create one of the most successful film franchises in the history of the movies? Like all great men, he came from comparatively modest beginnings - literally. For the town he was born in was Modesto, California...

The man himself, George Lucas

2
A Long Time Ago...

George Walton Lucas Jr, to give him his full name, was born on 14 May 1944. America, of course, was still in the grip of war at the time, though life in the small town of Modesto was relatively unaffected by the events in Europe. George Sr continued to run the town's stationery store, whilst his wife Dorothy concentrated on bringing up George Jr and his two older sisters Katy and Ann (a third sister, Wendy, would arrive in 1947).

Other local businesses continued their day to day activities unaffected, too, among them the Gallo winemaking company and several walnut farms. To say the least, things were pretty tranquil in Modesto. A great place to retire to, perhaps, but a little dull for youngsters looking for fun.

There was always the cinema, and 1944 produced some classics, among them *Laura, Double Indemnity* and *Meet Me in St Louis*. John Wayne, meanwhile, continued to fight the war single-handedly in *Back to Bataan*, though the year's big hit was unquestionably the Bing Crosby heartwarmer *Going My Way*, which earned seven Oscars. As the young George grew up, however, it was the Saturday morning serials that would prove to be of main interest to him. Both at the cinema and on local television, his favourites being *Tailspin Tommy* and *Flash Gordon*, the sci-fi elements of which would have an effect on his later career.

Akira Kurosawa with executive producers Francis Ford Coppola and
George Lucas on location for *Kagemusha*.

Celluloid fantasies and comic books aside, there was little in the way of
diversion in Modesto. At school, where he was a barely average student, Lucas
was the archetypal loner. Both skinny and introspective, he wasn't the sporting
type. Yet like the seven stone weakling who takes up the Charles Atlas
bodybuilding course after having sand kicked in his face, he'd have the last
laugh on those who bullied him in the school yard.

Drawing, photography and modelmaking proved to be early interests for the
young Lucas. Mostly solitary activities, he pursued these hobbies - a sign of the
creativity yet to come - in the privacy of his bedroom, as much to escape the
stern rantings of his father as much as anything else. As he moved into his teens,
however, it was cars that became his overriding main interest, and at the age of
fifteen his father, in a moment of hitherto unknown generosity, bought him a

Fiat Bianchina, into which Lucas poured much time, effort and money.

His car became the centre of Lucas's universe, and the time he spent cruising up and down Modesto's main street in it would, like his passion for comic books and serials, have a profound effect on his later creative output. Lucas now entered the world of burger bars, slicked back hair and leather jackets. He may have looked incongruous in the biker's uniform given his slight build, yet Lucas quickly fitted in with one of the town's gangs.

His passion for cars soon turned to racing, and to finance this, Lucas began working at a local garage. He also became a familiar face in the race pit crews around California, as well as at fairground racetracks. At this stage he even began to harbour aspirations to be a great driver. George Sr had other ideas, however, his goal being that his son would one day take over the family stationery business. Given his increasingly poor grades in school, the now eighteen-year-old Lucas would at least be guaranteed a job this way, yet a life in stationery couldn't have interested him less.

Lucas was saved the embarrassment of failing his final exams by an event that would change his life. Returning home from studying in the library, his car was involved in a crash with another vehicle. Though he was thrown free of his car, Lucas suffered internal injuries, and for a while it was touch and go that he would pull through. Over four months of recuperation followed, during which Lucas re-assessed his life. The thrill of speed would remain, yet it would be superseded by another passion. Moviemaking.

3
New Directions

Given his poor performance at high school, Lucas now threw himself into his studies with renewed enthusiasm. Two years at Modesto Junior College followed, where he majored in social sciences, his main areas of interest being psychology and anthropology. He also took a writing course, and at one stage seemed certain to pursue English at San Francisco State. However, he decided instead to try the entrance exams for USC at the urging of cinematographer Haskel Wexler, whom he had befriended through his interest in racing. The year was 1964 and Wexler had already made a name for himself photographing such films as *The Hoodlum Priest* (for director Irvin Kershner, who would later helm *The Empire Strikes Back*) and *America, America* (for the legendary Elia Kazan). Lucas took Wexler's advice, passed the exam and entered the world of student filmmaking.

Funded by a monthly allowance from his father, along with a part time job as a ticket taker at Disneyland, Lucas began to study film in all its aspects. From a viewer's point of view, he expanded his horizons by taking in European and Eastern arthouse movies, among them those by Fellini, Antonioni, Godard and Kurosawa. From a practical point, he first tackled animation, making good use of his drawing and graphic skills. The end result was a one minute short titled

15

Look at Life, which his tutor entered in several festivals.

Next Lucas turned his attention to live action projects, in which he developed his direction, photography and, most of all, his editing skills. Seven further short films followed, among them *1:42:08*, which followed the speed trials of a yellow racing car, and *Herbie*, an abstract study of a Volkswagen. Lucas was quickly turning into one of USC's most accomplished students, no mean feat given that fellow classmates included John Milius, Hal Barwood, Matthew Robbins, Walter Murch and Howard Kazanjian, all of whom would go on to have successful careers in Hollywood (indeed, Kazanjian would go on to co-executive produce *Raiders of the Lost Ark* with Lucas).

Lucas finally graduated in 1966, but remained in academe as a teaching assistant to a class of US marine and navy cameramen. Not one to waste a readymade crew, Lucas took half the class to help make a film of his own. A sci-fi short, it went by the title *Electronic Labyrinth: THX 1138; 4HB*, and followed the attempts of a man to escape an underground world. The film impressed a lot of people and went on to win the third National Student Film Festival in 1967. Lucas was clearly beginning to make a name for himself. So much so that he was one of four student filmmakers chosen by producer Carl Foreman to make a short film centred round the production of his latest epic, a western titled *MacKenna's Gold*, which re-united J. Lee-Thompson and Gregory Peck, the director and star of Foreman's 1961 hit *The Guns of Navarone*.

Filmed in the desert, the movie was a big budget affair with a stellar supporting cast, among them Omar Sharif, Eli Wallach, Edward G. Robinson, Raymond Massey, Burgess Meredith, Telly Savalas, Lee J. Cobb, Anthony Quayle and Keenan Wynn. However, rather than concentrate his efforts on documenting the making of *MacKenna's Gold*, Lucas instead made a film about the desert itself. Titled *6.18.67*, it proved to be Foreman's favourite, despite initial misgivings that it had nothing to do with his own picture, and was played on PBS in a special highlighting the project and, of course, *MacKenna's Gold*, earning it some free publicity. Yet despite the cast and the arresting desert locations, *MacKenna's Gold* failed to impress audiences and critics alike, whilst Lucas himself apparently loathed the way money was frittered away on the location. The film was a prime example of the expensive, old style studio picture which was quickly pricing itself out of existence.

Following his experiences in the desert, Lucas earned himself a six month scholarship at Warner Bros., where he was free to roam the lot and observe whatever was being produced at the time. Ironically, the day Lucas arrived, Jack Warner, who had founded the studio in 1923 with his brothers Albert, Harry and Sam, left for retirement in Palm Springs, following a merger with Seven Arts. The old Hollywood which Warner epitomised was quickly dying out, soon to be taken over by a dynamic breed of young filmmakers, out to shatter convention and speak to their own generation via the likes of *Easy Rider*, *M*A*S*H* and *Mean Streets*. Though Warner Bros would release the ground-breaking *Bonnie and Clyde* that same year - a film older executives worryingly failed to see any artistic or commercial merit in - they were still pretty much entrenched in the old style of filmmaking. A prime example of this was the musical *Finian's Rainbow*, which was being shot on the backlot by a young whizzkid director named Francis Ford Coppola.

At the age of 27, Coppola, a UCLA graduate, had already written and directed two impressive low budget films: *Dementia 13* (aka *The Haunted and the Hunted*), which was an effective shocker about a series of axe murders which he'd made for B-movie king Roger Corman, and *You're a Big Boy Now*, a sex comedy featuring such established names as Elizabeth Hartman, Rip Torn, Tony Bill, Karen Black and Geraldine Page, who earned an Oscar nomination for her performance. Made for Warner Bros., this second film was a fairly freewheeling affair and was described by critic Judith Crist as being 'wonderfully photogenic'. Given his burgeoning reputation, further helped by scriptwriting duties on *This Property is Condemned* (also for Seven Arts) and *Is Paris Burning?*, the studio decided to put their latest big budget musical, *Finian's Rainbow*, into the young maverick's hands.

Unfortunately, whilst Coppola would go on to make some of the greatest films of the seventies (among them *The Godfather*, *The Conversation*, *The Godfather Part Two* and *Apocalypse Now*), this lumbering, old fashioned musical about a leprechaun's search for his pot of gold was just not Coppola's forté. The film's cast was certainly impressive: Fred Astaire (in his last musical role), Tommy Steele, Petula Clarke and Keenan Wynn. Yet Coppola was uninspired by the material, which was based on a 1947 Broadway success with songs by Burton Lane and Yip Harburg, the most memorable being *How Are Things in Glocca Mora?* He was also hidebound by the studio's ageing, old-style technicians, who were less than eager to try anything new or innovative. The end result was a charmless flop, one of several big budget musicals to die a death at the box office during this period.

Nevertheless, despite the film's shortcomings, Lucas turned up each day to

watch Coppola work. He quickly befriended the director and not long after became his personal assistant, whilst his classmate Howard Kazanjian acted as the film's second assistant director. During breaks in filming, Lucas and Coppola would discuss getting away from the Hollywood style of filmmaking. Not just a pipe dream, the two decided to carry out their musings. Consequently, after *Finian's Rainbow* had been completed, Coppola and Lucas went on the road with a small but select crew to make a low budget drama. Bankrolled by Warner Bros., it was titled *The Rain People*, and starred James Caan as Jimmie 'Killer' Kilgannon, a brain-damaged ex-football player who, whilst hitchhiking to West Virginia for a job, is picked up by Natalie Ravenna, a neurotic housewife, played by Shirley Knight, who is trying to escape the binds of domesticity.

Despite the enthusiasm of the cast and crew for the project, the finished film was something of a pretentious bore with too few moments of true inspiration ('...an overlong, brooding film incorporating some excellent photography,' commented *Variety*). As a learning experience, however, the film proved invaluable to Lucas, who worked as the film's assistant cameraman. He was also the film's production manager, and put in time with the art and sound departments. If all this wasn't enough, he also made a 40 minute documentary about the production. Shot on 16mm, Lucas called it *Filmmaker*, and it was hailed as an excellent record of Coppola at work.

In what spare time he had during the making of *The Rain People*, Lucas also began to turn his student film, *Electronic Labyrinth: THX 1138; 4EB*, into a feature-length script. Using his chutzpah, Coppola had managed to wrangle a contract out of Warner Bros. for Lucas to develop his idea. His first commercial feature was gradually becoming a reality.

In the meantime, Coppola's long-held dream of running his own studio was also taking shape. Again, he managed to get the seemingly ever-benevolent Warner Bros to finance the project, which involved setting up a post-production facility in a warehouse in the less than salubrious Folsom Street district of San Francisco, conveniently away from Hollywood interference. As well as Coppola and Lucas, many of their USC and UCLA buddies made use of the equipment Coppola had bought (including a state-of-the-art sound editing suite). Called American Zoetrope, the company - and Coppola - was set for a stormy future.

Low-budget film-maker and mentor Roger Corman in action

Things were shaping up quickly for Lucas, too. He continued to gain experience in a variety of jobs, working for a while as a camera assistant for title designer Saul Bass. He also helped to photograph the Rolling Stones' free Altamont Speedway concert film *Gimme Shelter* (which was released in 1970), at which Hell's Angels, working as security guards, killed a member of the audience.

Then, on 22 February 1969, George Lucas married Marcia Griffin, an editor whom he met whilst doing some post production work on a US Information Agency documentary. The film was being supervised by Verna Fields, the legendary editor who would later go on to win an Oscar for her work on Steven Spielberg's *Jaws*. After an uncertain beginning, the romance between Lucas and Griffin developed quickly, and the couple decided that, rather than be continually working apart on different projects, they would get married and set up a home, complete with their own editing suite, where they could work at their convenience. Deciding upon Marin County, just outside San Francisco, as the perfect base, they found a house in Mill Valley and converted the loft into an editing suite.

Career-wise, Coppola's efforts on behalf of Lucas were also beginning to pay off. *THX: 1138*, as it was now called, was finally a go project with Warner Bros. There was also interest in an idea for a war epic that Lucas and John Milius had been batting about. This would eventually develop into *Apocalypse Now*, but wouldn't see the light of a movie projector for nearly another ten years. Thus Lucas channelled all his efforts into his debut feature. He was about to enter the big time.

4
Action!

THX stands for Tomlinson Holman's Experiment, Holman being the inventor of the THX sound system.

Lucas finally licked his *THX* script into shape with Walter Murch, whose services he also used to design the film's sound. The shooting schedule eventually ran to a somewhat lengthy forty days. Though Lucas and his crew may have had plenty of time to film *THX*, the budget, a tight $777,000 of which just $15,000 went to Lucas, was another matter. So, to avoid the cost of building futuristic sets, the director made much use of multi-storey parking lots and the tunnels of San Francisco's part-finished BART subway system, to help create the bleak look he was striving for.

The final story, which plays like a cross between *1984* and *This Perfect Day*, centres round THX: 1138, a lab technician living and working in a sterile, underground society governed by OMM, an Orwellian body whose robotic policemen and constant surveillance ensure that the citizens work hard and take the drugs that keep them docile and subdued. THX falls in love with his room mate, LUH;3417, however, and together they decide to stop taking their drugs, indulge in a little sexual activity and have a baby, all of which is of course strictly against OMM's rules. When the couple are found out, THX is sent to prison, which takes the form of an inescapable and seemingly never-ending white limbo. But escape he does, emerging from the labyrinth of tunnels into the warm glow of a setting sun.

To play THX, Lucas cast 39-year old Robert Duvall, an emerging star who had played the cop who takes up with Shirley Knight's character in Coppola's *Rain People*. Duvall's best work was yet to come, most notably in Coppola's *Godfather*, *Godfather Part Two* and *Apocalypse Now* (in which he got to say the immortal line, 'I love the smell of napalm in the morning. It smells of victory'). His performance in *THX: 1138* was more than adequate, however, perfectly capturing the soul-destroying conformity of life in Lucas's sterile future. He was also ably supported by Maggie McOmie as his love interest LUH: 3417, and genre favourite Donald Pleasence, whose character SEN: 5241 reports the misdemeanours of THX and LUH to the authorities. Also to be found in the cast were Ian Wolfe (a character actor familiar from such classics as *Mr Blandings Builds His Dream House* and *The Great Caruso*) and, way down the list, Johnny Weissmuller Jr as one of the chrome-faced robots.

Given the film's clinical look, along with the overall lack of human warmth on display, *THX: 1138* doesn't always make for easy viewing. Technically, however, there is much of interest on display. Lucas's direction of the action sequences is sharp and inventive without showing off, whilst his editing is tight without be overly slick. Lalo Schifrin's music score, most of it purposely bland background muzak, again to keep the citizens relaxed and docile, also adds to the film's impact, as does Walter Murch's inventive sound montages and Michael Haller's Spartan art direction. Another of Lucas's USC buddies, Hal Barwood, also contributed to the film, providing the titles.

Despite everybody's best efforts, however, the film failed to find an audience, and whilst some of the reviews were appreciative, the executives at Warner Bros. hated the movie. So much so they even lopped five minutes out of it before releasing it, much to Lucas's consternation.

With one commercial failure behind him, Lucas's future as a director was looking a little uncertain. He quickly needed to establish himself commercially. To do this, he decided it was time to indulge in a little warm-hearted nostalgia.

5
Happy Days

The licence plate on the car of John Milner (Paul LeMat) is THX 1138.

'Where were you in '62?'. So ran the poster tag line for Lucas's next picture, *American Graffiti*, the movie that finally put him on the map. A nostalgic comedy-drama shot in and around San Rafael in California, the story follows the last-night adventures of high school graduate Curt Henderson who, the next day, is to leave the town for college in the east. Full of doubt about his future, Henderson spends much of the movie searching for an elusive girl in a white T-Bird. Through him we also meet a variety of his friends and former schoolmates, all of them out cruising for girls up and down the town's main street. Obviously based on Lucas's own teenage experiences, the film benefited enormously from the writer-director's first-hand experience.

Lucas first managed to interest United Artists in the story, securing a $10 000 development deal from executive David Picker, whom he met whilst at the Cannes Film Festival in France, where he had travelled with Marcia, at their own expense, to promote *THX: 1138*, which had been selected to be a part of the Directors' Fortnight.

Once back home, Lucas mapped out the story with Willard Huyck and Huyck's writing partner wife, Gloria Katz. Unfortunately, other writing commitments meant that Huyck and Katz were unable to work on the actual screenplay, which Lucas subsequently handed - along with the $10 000 development fee - to Richard Walters. Sadly, both Lucas and Picker were disappointed with Walters' efforts, and so United Artists passed on the movie. Lucas next took the idea to Columbia, who also decided to pass. Finally, the story found a home at Universal, where Lucas's new producer, Gary Kurtz, managed to get it an all important green light.

Born in 1940, Kurtz was four years older than Lucas, and like his new associate, he was a USC graduate, having studied production, direction, editing and photography. He also had a strong interest in film, which stemmed back to his childhood, when he made 8mm movies, which he also edited and acted in. Also like Lucas, he loved the old movie serials, especially *Flash Gordon*.

Once he'd graduated from USC, Kurtz stayed on, working on a variety of projects, among them several US Public Health Service medical information shorts. He also ran the university's film lab. He then gained much practical experience in the professional world of moviemaking by joining producer Roger Corman's outfit where, over a four year period, he worked on dozens of low budgeters, holding such varied jobs as camera grip and sound recordist, as well as production manager and director. One of these pictures was the 1963 shocker *The Terror*, which Corman had hastily put into production over a weekend when he discovered there were a couple of days left to go on the contract he had with Boris Karloff, who had just starred in *The Raven* for him with Vincent Price, Peter Lorre and the young Jack Nicholson.

It was all hands to the pumps with *The Terror*. Jack Nicholson returned to flesh out the cast, which also included Sandra Knight, Dorothy Neumann and Corman regulars Dick Miller and Jonathan Haze (Seymour Krelboined in the original *Little Shop of Horrors*). Corman directed all the scenes involving the principals in just two days. Other sequences were then added to the film over the following months, among them one filmed at Big Sur involving Jack Nicholson and Sandra Knight, which was directed by Francis Ford Coppola, who was also the film's associate producer. It was during the filming of *The Terror* that Gary Kurtz met Coppola. The two hit it off straight away, and Coppola would later prove useful in helping Kurtz.

In the meantime, though, Kurtz's developing career was temporarily brought to a halt by the draft. Kurtz was drafted into the marines, became a camerman and went all over the world photographing raids and flying missions. It was *Apocalypse Now* for real, and Kurtz was right in the middle of it.

Upon his return to America, Kurtz resumed his career, working as an associate producer on *Two Lane Blacktop*, an *Easy Rider* wannabe road movie directed by Monte Hellman (who, coincidentally, had also directed several sequences for *The Terror*), and *Chandler*, a private eye drama, both of which were released in 1971. It was whilst prepping *Two Lane Blacktop* that Kurtz finally met George Lucas. Monte Hellman wanted to shoot the movie in Techniscope, and Kurtz was sent to find out about the process. He first approached his friend Francis Ford Coppola for advice, who in turn sent him to see Lucas, who had just shot *THX: 1138* in the process. Lucas was editing *THX* at the time, and the two hit it off.

When the opportunity for the duo to work together finally arose, it was *Apocalypse Now* that was first seriously considered as a project. Kurtz even travelled to the Philippines to scout locations, but eventually the idea was shelved (again) for being too expensive. Kurtz and Lucas also toyed with an idea for a Flash Gordon sci-fi adventure, which was also put on the back burner, as the rights, owned by King Features, were also financially out of their league. Eventually they decided upon Lucas's nostalgia piece, which they finally managed to find a home for at Universal, for whom Kurtz had worked on *Two Lane Blacktop*. Part of the deal involved Francis Ford Coppola producing the movie with Kurtz. At the time, Coppola was on the cusp of releasing *The Godfather* on the world. Word of mouth already had the film touted as a blockbuster, and Coppola's name on the *American Graffiti* credits would give the picture a little extra gravitas, given that it would have no star names in the cast. Lucas and Kurtz agreed and the movie was given the go-ahead.

Again, the budget was tight, just $850,000, of which Lucas received $20 000. The shooting schedule was even tighter; a scant 28 days, most of which would be spent on location in such places as Bakersfield, Marin County, Pinole, San Rafael, Sonoma County and Petaluma.

By now, Lucas's script had been through several drafts. Indeed, so much time had elapsed since he, Willard Huyck and Gloria Katz had mapped out the original story, the couple had finished the other script they had been hired to write, so they returned to work on *American Graffiti* with Lucas.

There was also the matter of casting. Coppola advised that Lucas work with Fred Roos in that respect. Roos had helped Coppola cast much of *The Godfather* and would later go on to help produce such movies as *The Godfather*

Part Two, Apocalypse Now, One from the Heart and *The Cotton Club*.

The casting process took many months and involved over one-hundred-and-fifty auditions. Among those cast were Richard Dreyfus, who took the leading role of Curt Henderson. Dreyfus would of course go on to become one of the biggest stars of the seventies and eighties in the like of *Jaws, Close Encounters* and *Down and Out in Beverly Hills*, though at this stage in his career his movie resume just amounted to brief appearances in *The Graduate, Hello Down There, The Young Runaways, Dillinger* (which had been written and directed by Lucas's USC classmate John Milius) and *The Second Coming of Suzanne*. *American Graffiti* would be his big break.

Also in the cast were former child star Ron Howard, who played Steve Bolander, Henderson's buddy, also set to leave for college. Familiar from such movies as *The Music Man* and *The Courtship of Eddie's Father*, as well as such popular TV shows as *The Andy Griffith Show* and *The Smith Family*, Howard would go on to become a respected director, helming such movies as *Splash, Cocoon, Backdraft* and *Apollo 13*. His association with Lucas would also continue beyond *American Graffiti*, with Howard directing *Willow* for Lucas in 1988. His performance as the up-beat Steve in *American Graffiti* would remain his best work as an actor.

Other up-coming names hired to flesh out the characters included Paul LeMat who played greaser John Milner, said to be loosely based on Lucas's pal John Milius. Milner spends much of the movie cruising in his souped-up 1932 Ford Deuce Coupe (license plate THX 1138 coincidentally), said to be the fastest car in the valley. Unfortunately, his attempts at finding a shapely date are seriously hampered when he picks up thirteen-year-old Carol (Mackenzie Phllips), at first mistakenly believing her to be older. Milner finds himself lumbered with the mouthy teenager for the rest of the evening, and their subsequent banter provides plenty of comic clashes.

For the role of Curt Henderson's sister Laurie, Lucas hired Cindy Williams. In the movie, Debbie is dating Curt's buddy Steve, and her fears for the future add a touch of poignancy to the proceedings. As the resident dork Terry 'the Toad' Fields, Lucas chose Charles Martin Smith. The young actor added many comic moments to the movie in his woebegone attempts to be cool, the best of them involving him crashing his moped into a coke machine early on in the movie, providing an ice-breaking belly laugh for the audience.

Candy Clark, as flirty blonde Debbie, was also featured strongly. She had just worked for director John Huston on *Fat City*, which had also been cast by Fred

Roos. Other up-coming names were included too, among them Bo Hopkins, who had become a familiar face via such westerns as *The Wild Bunch*, *Monte Walsh* and *The Culpepper Cattle Company*; legendary disc jockey Wolfman Jack (real name Robert Smith), whom Curt has a memorable encounter with towards the end of the movie; future *Three's Company* sit-com star Suzanne Somers as Curt's T-Bird fantasy girl; and Kathleen Quinlan, who would later become familiar from her Joe Dante-directed segment in *Twilight Zone: The Movie* and her Oscar-nominated performance in Ron Howard's *Apollo 13*.

Another soon-to-be-familiar name further down the cast list was Harrison Ford who, as Bob Falfa, challenges John Milner to a car race at the movie's climax. The role was a small but telling one which Ford made his own. Ford would of course go on to much bigger things with Lucas, and at this stage of his career was just a jobbing actor like the rest of the young cast, earning just $500 a week for *American Graffiti*. In fact he supplemented his acting jobs with work as a carpenter, which is how he'd met casting director Fred Roos.

Born in 1942, Ford had been acting since 1964, when he made his stage debut with The Belfry Players. His rise to the top of the industry was a particularly long and arduous one, though, and at several stages seemed doomed to failure. Following his time with The Belfry Players, Ford did a season of summer stock at the Laguna Beach Playhouse, which is where a talent spotter for Columbia saw him and signed him to their talent programme. Things seemed on the up for Ford. However, acting classes and photo shoots aside, the resultant film appearances were minor and of little value to him. His movie debut came in *Dead Heat on a Merry-go-Round*, a disappointing caper comedy in which, as a bell boy, he had a brief scene with the film's star, James Coburn.

A couple of more insignificant roles followed in *Luv* and *A Time for Killing* (aka *The Long Ride Home*), after which Ford, dissatisfied with Columbia, left for a new contract with Universal. Here he got plenty of guest shots on such established shows as *The Virginian*, *Gunsmoke*, *The Partridge Family* and *Kung Fu*. There was also another movie, *Journey to Shiloh*, and loan-outs to appear in *Getting Straight* (for Columbia, ironically) and *Zabriskie Point*. Ford's career was getting nowhere fast, and following a role in a minor TV movie western, *The Intruders*, he took to carpentry, which he'd originally done so to renovate his house, and more or less quit acting. It was in his capacity as a chippie that Ford met Fred Roos, who filed his face away for future use, and the rest, as they say, is history.

Following the weeks of preparation, filming on *American Graffiti* finally commenced in June 1972. Like most movies there were problems here and there. After complaints were received from locals about the disruption filming was causing early in the shoot, Lucas switched locations from San Rafael to Petaluma. Some of the ageing cars used in the movie also proved to be temperamental, while the continuous night shooting was a tiring experience for all concerned. Otherwise, everyone slogged away, determined to bring the film in on time and budget (in fact so tight was the budget, Harrison Ford received a reprimand during a coffee break for eating two doughnuts instead of the allotted one!).

As with the cast, the crew was also young and eager, among them cinematographers Jan D'Alquen and Ron Eveslage, art director Al Locatelli, who came up with some striking locations, most notably Mel's Diner, around which much of the action is set, and costume designer Aggie Guerrard Rodgers, whose uniforms for the diner's roller-skating carhops were particularly eye-catching. Lucas's friend, cinematographer Haskell Wexler, who by now had photographed such hits as *Who's Afraid of Virginia Woolf?* (for which he'd won an Oscar), *In the Heat of the Night* and *The Thomas Crown Affair*, was also on hand as a visual consultant. The film's complex editing, obviously supervised by Lucas, was meanwhile in the assured hands of Marcia Lucas and Verna Fields who, as well as keeping the pacing tight, had to liaise carefully with sound editor Walter Murch, who had the job of inserting forty-four pop songs from the era into the soundtrack.

In an inspired move, Lucas decided to forego the traditional orchestral soundtrack and instead add to the film's atmosphere with such hits as *Why Do Fools Fall in Love?* by Frankie Lymon, *Chantilly Lace* by The Big Bopper, *Only You* by The Platters, *Johnny B. Goode* by Chuck Berry, *That'll Be the Day* by Buddy Holly and *Rock Around the Clock* by Bill Haley and His Comets. It cost $80,000 to purchase the rights to the various numbers for the movie, but this proved a sound investment, for when the picture became a hit, sales of the resultant album skyrocketed, making it the father of the pop soundtrack tie-in, selling 100,000 in its first two weeks of release.

But that was still some time away. When filming was finally completed, cast and crew wrapped with a fifties-style party at Art Laboe's rock revival club on Sunset Strip. Then, in the following months, Lucas dedicated himself to the film's post production. By the end of January 1973 he delivered his director's cut, which was then screened at a Northpoint theatre for Universal executive Ned Tannen and a specially invited audience on Sunday 21 January.

The film went down a storm with the younger members of the audience, yet astonishingly, Tannen hated the movie. When it was over he began to rant at Lucas, Kurtz and Coppola, much to their shock. Coppola gave back as good as Tannen dished out, however, and even offered to buy the movie back from Universal. Over the next few days various ideas as to what to do with the movie were batted about, including releasing it direct to television and re-titling it *Another Slow Night in Modesto*. In the end Tannen, once he'd calmed down, decided that a little re-cutting might help matters.

As far as Lucas was concerned, this was sacrilege, especially after his similar experiences with *THX* at Warner Bros.. To be honest, the alterations ordered by Tannen weren't too drastic, and following several more successful studio screenings, the film was released theatrically in August 1973. Despite the problems with Tannen and the studio, Lucas had the last laugh, for the film was an instant hit. Lucas had hoped that it might make $10m. Ultimately it went on to gross a staggering $117m worldwide, of which $55m came from America alone. After tax, Lucas's share of the profits was a hefty $4m.

A sleeper hit hailed as the quintessential study of teenage life in the sixties, it also garnered some great reviews. 'Masterfully executed and profoundly affecting,' commented *The LA Times*, to which *Variety* added, 'American Graffiti is one of those rare films which can be advanced in any discussion of the superiority of film over live performance. The latter can vary from show to show, but if you get it right on film, you've got it forever.'

In addition to the critical plaudits and the box office success, *American Graffiti* also did pretty well on the awards circuit, winning the New York Film Critics' Award and the National Society of Film Critics Award for best screenplay. It also garnered a Golden Globe for best musical/comedy picture, plus a second Golden Globe for Paul LeMat as best male newcomer. In February 1974, when the all-important Academy Award nominations were announced, *American Graffiti* was present in five categories: best picture (Kurtz and Coppola), best director (Lucas), best original story and screenplay (Lucas, Huyck and Katz), best editing (Marcia Lucas and Verna Fields) and best supporting actress (Candy Clark).

Surprisingly, the film didn't earn a nomination for Walter Murch's brilliant sound design. It also failed to win in any of its categories, losing best picture to *The Sting* (but then so did *Cries and Whispers*, *The Exorcist* and *A Touch of Class*, so the company was honourable). Meanwhile, Lucas lost best director to George Roy Hill for *The Sting*; best original story and screenplay went to David

Oscar competition for Lucas: George Roy Hill directs
Paul Newman and Robert Redford in *The Sting*.

S. Ward for *The Sting*; best editing went to William Reynolds, also for *The Sting*; and the best supporting actress gong went to the young Tatum O'Neal for *Paper Moon*.

Given the film's huge success, disappointment at the Oscars didn't seem to matter too much. Lucas was now financially secure, thanks to the deal he brokered when signing to make *American Graffiti*, which he did so through his own film company, Lucasfilm. So things were looking decidedly rosy, even if Universal's handling of the movie still smarted. The question now was, what was Lucas's next project going to be? He had to prove he wasn't just a one hit wonder. *American Graffiti* may have earned him a place in the history books. His next film would completely re-write them.

6

Keep Watching the Skies

The surprise runaway success of *American Graffiti* had established George Lucas as one of the industry's most exciting filmmakers. Not only was he now a multi-millionaire, he also found himself being feted by the Hollywood studios, all keen for him to produce another hit for them. Given his struggles with both *THX: 1138* at Warner Bros. and *American Graffiti* at Universal - both of which had been tampered with - Lucas found all the attention a little disconcerting. So as the offers began to flood in, Lucas sat back a little. He had $4m in the bank. There was no need to rush into something not worth his while. And there was always his *Flash Gordon*/sci-fi idea to keep him occupied.

In fact the roots of *Star Wars*, as his sci-fi project would eventually come to be called, could be found in Lucas's work on the aborted production of *Apocalypse Now*, for which he'd wanted to develop the theme of a low-tech rebellion beating a powerful high-tech force. The film that Francis Ford Coppola finally made differed quite dramatically from this concept. Nevertheless, Lucas retained the idea, which he gradually shaped as the central theme of *Star Wars*.

Work on the *Star Wars* script officially began in April 1973, with Lucas sketching out the various plotlines. Particularly inspired by the fan mail he'd been receiving from youngsters about *American Graffiti*, Lucas was determined to make another film for this audience. The United States was heavily involved in the Vietnam war at the time, and Lucas wanted to make a positive and inspiring film for teenagers and children. The occasional Disney film aside, few films of the kind that Lucas had grown up with - serials, westerns, pirate movies, adventures - were being made for this target audience. The last truly great science fiction films had been made in the late sixties, and though *Planet of the Apes* and *2001* had both been spectacularly successful, they weren't particularly geared towards kids.

That said, if Lucas was going to make a *Flash Gordon*-style adventure, he didn't want it to be camp, or poke knowing fun at itself. He wanted kids to accept the adventures for real, and so decided to restrict the movie's humour. Thus, taking his inspiration from *Flash*, he sat down and began to research where the superhero's creator, Alex Raymond, had got his own ideas from. This led him to the works of Edgar Rice Boroughs and Edwin Arnold. He also delved into mythology, reading Joseph Campbell's *Hero with a Thousand Faces*. He even went as far as meeting Campbell and fellow mythologist Bruno Bettelheim.

He gained further inspiration from Frank Herbert's *Dune*, Carlos Castaneda's *Tales of Power*, Isaac Asimov's *Foundation* trilogy, C.S. Lewis's *Chronicles of Narnia*, J.R.R. Tolkein's *Lord of the Rings* and the fairytales of the Brothers Grimm. Movie-wise, he watched the likes of *The Thief of Baghdad*, *The Sea Hawk*, *Captain Blood* and the Nazi propaganda documentary *Triumph of the Will*. He also took note that Flash Gordon had two side kicks, one male (Dr Zarkov) and one female (Dale Arden). The planet Mongo meanwhile helped to inspire a setting, whilst the nefarious deeds of Ming the Merciless gave him a few ideas concerning a chief villain. He also researched into the film's prospective budget, figuring that the movie could make $16m on a $4.5m outlay if bolstered by a hefty advertising campaign.

By the middle of May 1973, Lucas had an outline down on paper, though nothing was concrete. The story would continue to evolve over the next few months. Initially, the film was to be set in the 23rd century. A princess-in-peril story as recalled by a character called Mace Windu, it involved the rescue of royal Princess Leia Aguilae from the Black Knight Valarium by General Luke Skywalker and a fellow Jedi Knight called Annakin Starkiller. Other characters involved included another evil knight, General Darth Vader, a pilot, Han Solo, and two comical robots. There were space battles in Devil Fighter planes, a chase through an asteroid field and giant winged creatures. The tale ended with the Princess revealing that she is in fact a demi-god.

The idea for the Jedi Knights had come from director Akira Kurosawa's *Seven Samurai*, in which sixteenth-century villagers hire seven samurai to defend their village against bandits. Lucas derived the word Jedi the Japanese words jidai geki, a phrase meaning period drama. Another of Kurosawa's movies, *The Hidden Fortress*, in which an heiress is saved from a bandit by a samurai, also inspired Lucas. Indeed, the film's star, Toshiro Mifune, is said to be the basis for Obi-Wan Kenobi, another character Lucas now added to the story.

At the same time Lucas was buried in his *Star Wars* script, Francis Ford Coppola decided to again resurrect *Apocalypse Now*, his hope being to have the movie ready as part of America's bi-centennial celebrations. The movie was still Lucas's if he wanted it, but he preferred to remain with *Star Wars*. Coppola thus re-wrote the story with John Milius and went on to direct it himself. The production was a lengthy and troubled one, and though the resultant movie, which didn't appear on screen until 1979, was hailed a classic, Lucas felt the film's story was unfaithful to his original idea.

The treatment Lucas had finished in May was now being sent round the studios. Universal and United Artists were the first ports of call, but both decided to pass Lucas's offer to write and direct the movie for a $25,000 fee. They couldn't understand the script, thinking it too full of weird names and incidents. They also doubted whether the effects could be pulled off. Given his problems with Universal, Lucas was no doubt glad the studio passed. With the benefit of hindsight, we can now view these rejections as the biggest mistakes in the history of both studios, all of which must have given Lucas some pleasure later. Instead, at the urging of his new friend Steven Spielberg, Lucas asked his agent, Jeff Berg, to send the treatment to Twentieth Century Fox for the attention of a new executive called Alan Ladd, Jr., the son of the legendary star of such classics as *This Gun For Hire*, *The Blue Dahlia* and *Shane*.

A former talent agent, Ladd began producing in the early seventies, making such movies as *The Nightcomers* and *Fear is the Key* in England. When Fox hit troubled waters following a number of costly flops, among them *Doctor Dolittle*, *Hello, Dolly!* and *Tora! Tora! Tora!*, Ladd was hired by the studio's head of production, Jere Henshaw, to help revitalize the company and steer it towards more audience-friendly pictures.

With this in mind, Ladd arranged for Lucas to come and see him at Fox to 'pitch' his treatment. So enthusiastic was Lucas about his story, Ladd became instantly interested in the space opera. As the meeting progressed, the two also discussed their favourite movies, and Ladd admitted to having enjoyed both *American Graffiti* and even *THX: 1138*. Lucas had finally met someone with similar enthusiasms. He was also impressed by Ladd's honesty. Finally, the two shook hands and agreed to let their lawyers sort out an initial deal. Consequently, Lucas received $10,000 to develop his story into a full script, with the promise of another $50,000 if the studio agreed to go ahead with the movie. Lucas's involvement as a director would add another $100,000 to his package. A prospective production budget of $3.5m was also mentioned.

The success of *American Graffiti* had meant that Lucas and his wife could now afford to buy a larger home, which they did, purchasing a Victorian mansion in San Anselmo. They called the place Parkhouse, and added to it the pre-requisite editing suite plus a screening room. It was at Parkhouse that Lucas would spend the next eighteen months further developing the storyline of *Star Wars*, which at the time was titled *The Story of Mace Windu*.

Always with a notepad by his side, Lucas disciplined himself into working eight hours a day on the script, writing, re-writing, remoulding and shaping it until he felt he had what he wanted. The story's theme remained consistent - good versus evil - but characters and incidents came and went.

Lucas completed his first draft in May 1974. By this time he realised that his film would have more impact and appeal to audiences if he changed his hero warrior, General Luke Skywalker, to a novice youth, and so concocted a version of the story centred round an eighteen-year-old Annakin Skywalker and his older brother Biggs, who together rescue their father from the clutches of the perfidious emperor. The brothers also take on Prince Valarium, the Black Knight of the Sith, and a grim imperial general named Darth Vader. Along the way, the brothers encounter Owen Lars, an anthropologist specialising in Wookiee customs, and two battered robots called R2-D2 (a name Lucas had derrived from the technical term reel two, dialogue two) and C-3PO. There was also a green-hued beast with gills thrown in for good measure!

By July, Anakin Skywalker had become Justin Valor, Princess Leia had become Zara, the Wookiees had become Jawas and Valarium was now a Jedi hunter called Captain Dodona. Feeling things were now getting muddled, Lucas carried on working, and by January 1975 he'd added more mysticism to the proceedings. He also added a quest for the legendary Kiber Crystal, a Force-

34

channeling shard. This Force was divided into good and evil, the good side known as The Ashla, the bad as The Bogan.

At this stage the script was called *The Adventures of the Starkiller, Episode One of the Star Wars* and the plot now involved the rescue of Luke Starkiller's brother, Deak, from the cloud city of Alderaan. The Dark Side is represented by Prince Espaa Valorum, Master of the Bogan, and his two henchmen Darklighter and Darth Vader. The story also involved a Correllian smuggler called Han Solo, who has a furry alien girlfriend called Boma. Solo's crew included a character called Jabba the Hutt. There was also a seer called Ben, who guides Luke Starkiller telepathically from afar. A rebel general called Tarkin was now part of the action, too, along with imperial troopers called Tusken. The whole script finally concluded with a teaser for the next episode - the Lars family is kidnapped and a perilous search begins for their cousin Leia.

Among the highlights of this script was a climax set on a jungle planet called Yarvin, which is populated by the Wookiees. There is also an Imperial base on the planet. Luke fights the head Wookiee, wins, but spares the creature's life. He then becomes the Wookiees' new leader and rallies them to attack the Imperial base. This done, the Wookiees are then trained by Han and Ben to fly and attack a Death Star. This finally accomplished, everyone celebrates with a big dance in the forest. Again, all this material was abandoned, only to resurface later, re-worked, as part of the third *Star Wars* film, *Return of the Jedi*. Nevertheless, Lucas loved the Wookiee concept, which he decided was a cross between a bear, a monkey and his pet dog Indiana, and so decided to make one Han Solo's second in command in his final draft. He called this Wookiee Chewbacca. Said to be 200 years old, he is a lovable creature - except when riled!

By this time, Lucas had enough material for three films, never mind one, so he decided to concentrate on the epic's first act, leaving aside many ideas to be developed in the two sequels. It was gradually becoming apparent that his script was centring round the adventures of the young Luke Skywalker who, like several of the characters in *American Graffiti*, had many of Lucas's own traits. Similarly, smuggler Han Solo was not unlike his buddy John Milius, whilst the two comical robots were seen as a variation on Laurel and Hardy.

By March 1975, Lucas had started in earnest to whittle down his epic story, originally some 500 pages long, to a more manageable length. By 1 August, he had more or less completed his task. The narrative was less ambitious and more linear and all the better for it. It also now contained a catchphrase, 'May the force be with you,' which became the equivalent of the Musketeers' cry of, 'All for one and one for all!'.

At this stage in the proceedings, Lucas and Gary Kurtz decided to invest $300,000 of their *American Graffiti* earnings into The Star Wars Corporation, to help further develop the movie. As and when they got the final green light from Fox to go ahead with the movie - which was no means a certainty - the two wanted to be as well prepared as possible. *Star Wars* was going to be a huge production, so the more time and effort they spent on pre-production the better.

To help visualize some of Lucas's concepts, they hired artist Ralph McQuarrie. A former illustrator for Boeing, Kaiser Graphics and CBS News (for which he'd illustrated the Apollo missions), McQuarrie was now making inroads as a production illustrator and storyboard artist. In fact it was Lucas's USC classmates Hal Barwood and Matthew Robbins who had introduced Lucas to McQuarrie a couple of years earlier, at which time McQuarrie was doing some work for them for a movie titled *Star Dance*, which ultimately never got made.

McQuarie's first job was to illustrate four key scenes from Lucas's script, to help put over the idea and look of the movie to Fox executives, who might not be able to imagine flights of interplanetary fancy. Thus McQuarrie illustrated robots R2-D2 and C-3P0 in the desert wastelands of Tatooine, the duel between Obi-Wan Kenobi and Darth Vader, stormtroopers firing, and the attack on the Death Star. It was an inspired idea. These concept paintings completed, McQuarrie and production illustrator Colin Cantwell (who'd worked on *2001*) then began to work on the initial design of spacecraft. McQuarrie based his sketches on the script and discussions with Lucas. Alex Tavoularis, the brother of Francis Ford Coppola's regular production designer, also began working on storyboards for the movie.

Work on the film's costumes was also undertaken at this stage. It was initially decided that the main characters would have tight-fitting outfits with distinctive collars and basic colours. The mystical Obi-Wan Kenobi was meanwhile given a habit in the style of a monk, whilst Princess Leia's costume, a flowing white robe, had a pre-Raphaelite air to it. As things progressed, Luke's clothes became baggier, whilst Han Solo's began to resemble a

Darth Vader and Carrie Fisher meet again during the last
re-launch of the original central *Star Wars* trilogy on video

36

gunslinger. Chewbacca was even given clothes at one stage until finally restricted to his trademark bandoleer. Darth Vader's mask, meanwhile, was based on the armour of a Samurai warrior, whilst his black flowing cape was based on the robes of the evil Jaffar (played by Conrad Veidt) in *The Thief of Baghdad*.

Determined for a realistic and feasible look at all times, Lucas insisted that his *Star Wars* universe should look lived-in rather than showroom fresh. Costumes would therefore be grubby and bashed about where necessary, whilst spacecraft would look as if they had actually flown thousands, if not millions, of miles across the galaxies.

Craft-wise, Han Solo's Millennium Falcon was said to have been inspired by a hamburger with an olive next to it, whilst its cockpit was based on the 'greenhouse' window of a B-29 Superfortress. The gun turrets were an adaptation of those found on a B-17 Flying Fortress. Meanwhile, the film's TIE fighter planes were initially called so because their shape resembles a bow tie, though TIE eventually became an acronym for Twin Ion Engines.

Eventually, the concept drawings for both costumes and spacecraft would fall into the hands of John Mollo and John Barry respectively. However, clothes and hardware were the least of Lucas and Kurtz's worries. Top of their pre-production agenda was the film's many and varied special effects and how they would be achieved convincingly - if at all!

7

Industrial Light and Magic

In order to bring the magical and hitherto unseen sights of *Star Wars* to the screen, Lucas and Kurtz came to the conclusion that there had to be something of a revolution in the effects industry. To bring this about, they turned, in June 1975, to John Dykstra, to help them.

Born in 1947, Dykstra was an up-and-coming light in the world of effects, having gained experience as an assistant to the great Douglas Trumbull, working for him on such movies as *The Andromeda Strain* and *Silent Running*, the latter of which Trumbull had also produced and directed. Dykstra, Lucas and Kurtz all came to the conclusion that if *Star Wars* was going to happen, new technology needed to be developed to achieve the effects required. With this in mind, they leased an old warehouse (at Van Nuys in Southern California's San Fernando Valley) in which to research and develop the technology required, tagging the facility The Industrial Light and Magic Corporation, a subsidiary of Lucasfilm.

Given the investment in the film's special effects, it was beginning to look increasingly unlikely that *Star Wars* could be made for the original estimate of $6.5m. Ultimately, some $2.5m would be spent on the effects alone. Once the building had been acquired at Van Nuys, John Dykstra began to get together a staff to help pull off the challenge. Eschewing Hollywood's old guard of effects technicians and their entrenched ways, he instead decided to employ younger film school students, college graduates, computer buffs and camera addicts who would make up for their lack of experience with enthusiasm and an eagerness to try and achieve the impossible. To help Dykstra in this task, Gary Kurtz hired his friend Jim Nelson, who would act as Industrial Light and Magic's production manager.

Kurtz also began to look into studio facilities around this time. Given Fox's increasing concerns about the budget for *Star Wars*, Kurtz needed to find studio space in which to film the movie that offered more competitive rates than those in Hollywood. A trip to Europe was thus arranged, and after touring studio space in Italy, France and Britain, Kurtz decided upon Elstree Studios just outside London. On the verge of closure, Elstree desperately needed the income a movie such as *Star Wars* would bring. Given this situation, Kurtz was able to negotiate a good deal, pencilling in a four month hire of the whole complex beginning in June 1976. The savings Kurtz made here would help bring down the budget for *Star Wars* quite considerably, all of which could only impress the Fox executives, who still had yet to decide whether the film was going to go ahead or not.

That go-ahead finally came in December 1975, following further meetings with Alan Ladd Jr and various Fox executives that began in October. Kurtz had proposed a carefully thought out budget of $10.5m, but Fox demurred, proposing $8m, as they believed the film not to be that great a commercial prospect. In fact the start-up budget was almost $200,000 short of the promised $8m, yet at least the film was now greenlighted. Surely, once the movie was well underway, Lucas and Kurtz could haggle for more money? Indeed, when Lucas and Kurtz threatened to take the movie away from Fox, they finally got the budget - more or less - that they required; a flat $10m

In negotiating the final contracts for the movie, Lucas was actually able to take some advantage of the fact that not everyone at Fox had faith in the movie. Consequently, Lucas and Kurtz negotiated away from Fox the sequel rights to *Star Wars*, along with the soundtrack and merchandising rights. Thinking these rights worthless, Fox agreed to let them go, ultimately at a cost of millions - nay, hundreds of millions - to the studio. As a fan of toys and games, Lucas wanted to create a movie with merchandising potential, and there was much in the *Star Wars* universe that could be exploited in this way. In addition to mugs and tee-shirts, Lucas wanted there to be *Star Wars* comic, along with models of the spacecraft, action figures and light swords. Like Fox, however, publishers and toy manufacturers at first were somewhat lukewarm about these ideas when approached.

To get the deals he wanted and to make the toy manufacturers and comic book publishers see the light, Lucas hired Charles Lippincott who, in addition to working on advertising, publicity and promotion for *Star Wars*, was also made vice-president of merchandising. Lippincott's first port of call was Marvel where, after much wrangling, he managed to secure a deal for a *Star Wars* comic with the company's chief executive Stan Lee, who himself had created Spiderman. Next, a deal was struck with publishers Ballantine for a novelization of the script to be written by Alan Dean Foster, to appear in the company's new Del Rey imprint.

While all this was going on, contract negotiations were finally coming to a close. Instead of negotiating extra money for himself at this stage for his writing and directing chores on the movie, it was mutually agreed that Lucas's Star Wars Corporation would instead get 40 percent of the net profits. Consequently, Lucas only got his flat $150,000 up front for his work, whilst Kurtz received $50,000. This was peanuts even in the mid seventies. However, if Fox thought they had got the duo cheap, Lucas and Kurtz would have the last laugh - big time.

With all the paperwork now sorted, the only thing left to do was actually go out and make the movie. So, whilst John Dykstra and his team continued to develop the technology needed to film the effects and Charles Lippincott continued to sublicense the merchandising, Lucas turned himself to the casting process. Having worked so successfully with unknowns on *American Graffiti*, Lucas again decided to go down this route again, so a huge call went out.

The casting of *Star Wars* would take some three months to complete. Lucas wanted personable actors who would basically be playing extensions of themselves. Thus agents were asked to send in character breakdowns of their clients when they submitted them for consideration. Casting calls are often nightmares for actors, as they have just a few minutes to make an impression on a director, and often have to read a few lines of dialogue cold. For the shy Lucas, the process was equally nightmarish. In an attempt to avoid having to talk to his prospective cast too much, the director decided to hold his auditions in the same room that his friend Brian de Palma was casting his own next movie, *Carrie*.

Lucas wanted to avoid casting the same actors he'd used in *American Graffiti*, though Richard Dreyfuss managed to get an audition for the role of Han Solo, as did Cindy Williams for Princess Leia. Other soon-to-be-famous names who Lucas saw included Peter Firth, Patrick Duffy, Bruce Boxleitner, William Katt (who would be cast in *Carrie*), Kurt Russell, Nick Nolte, Billy Dee Williams, Tom Berenger, Christopher Walken, Robby Benson and Frederic Forrest. Female considerations included Sissy Spacek (who would play the title role in *Carrie*), Jodie Foster, Jenny Agutter (who was making *Logan's Run* for MGM at the time), Amy Irving, Lisa Eilbacher and Penthouse Pet Terri Nunn. None of them seemed quite right to Lucas, however.

Then things gradually began to click. Fred Roos, who'd been asked again to provide some casting advice, contrived to have Harrison Ford work at Francis Ford Coppola's offices on a door during one set of auditions. Roos saw Ford as the perfect Han Solo. Following his work on *American Graffiti*, Ford's career had again slumped and he was relying increasingly on his skills as a carpenter to bring in money, despite occasional minor roles in the likes of *The Conversation* (directed by Coppola) and *The Court Martial of Lieutenant Calley* (a TV movie). Naturally, Ford felt a little ill-used at having to build a door whilst others auditioned for *Star Wars*. Eventually, though, Ford was asked in not only to read for the part, but also to read lines with other auditioning actors. These readings were videotaped, and everyone, Lucas included, decided that Ford was the best choice to play Solo, despite Lucas's edict that no one from *American Graffiti* would be cast.

Meanwhile, a young actor called Mark Hamill, who'd been to the *Star Wars/Carrie* sessions was recalled to read for Luke Skywalker (or Luke Starkiller, as he was then still known). Another unknown, Hamill had made his debut on TV's *Bill Cosby Show*, after which he'd appeared in episodes of *The Partridge Family* and *Cannon*. Following his video test, Hamill was recalled for a full screentest, which resulted in his being cast (ironically, he'd fallen through the net some years earlier, having auditioned for *American Graffiti*!). Similarly, the young Carrie Fisher, the daughter of Hollywood legend Debbie Reynolds and singer Eddie Fisher, had impressed during her readings with Harrison Ford. Like Ford and Hamill, her resume was limited (a brief but telling role in *Shampoo*, appearances in her mother's cabaret act), but it was her feisty

Carrie Fisher cuddles an Imperial Stormtrooper

personality that eventually won her the role of Princess Leia. Ford, Hamill and Fisher finally signed for the movie on 26 February 1976, just one month before shooting was to start in England. They would all be earning just $1000 per week each.

With so much untested talent onboard, Fox executive Alan Ladd Jr suggested that a couple of established names be added to the cast for marquee value. Lucas finally agreed and sent his script to Alec Guinness, who was then in Hollywood finishing off a Neil Simon comedy, *Murder by Death*. Though not a keen sci-fi fan, Guinness agreed to meet Lucas and was subsequently much impressed by him. One of the great British film stars, Guinness had appeared in such classics as *Oliver Twist*, *The Lavender Hill Mob*, *The Ladykillers* and *The Bridge on the River Kwai*, for which he'd won an Oscar. His presence in *Star Wars* would not only add a name value to the movie, but his aura would add immeasurably to the character of Obi-Wan Kenobi.

After many discussions, Guinness finally agreed to appear in the film towards the end of March, and though his fee was substantially lower than his usual asking price, part of his package involved a 2.25 percent share in the movie's profits. By 1997, it was estimated that Guinness had made $6m from the movie.

The rest of the casting was also being finalized around this time, too. Phil Brown was taken on to play Skywalker's uncle, Owen Lars, whilst his aunt Beru was handed to Shelagh Fraser. Meanwhile, to play the evil Grand Moff Tarkin, Lucas hired the revered British horror icon Peter Cushing, long a favourite with fans for his portrayals of Baron Frankenstein and Van Helsing. There was also the matter of finding people to play the many fully-costumed roles in the movie. Among them were Anthony Daniels, who was asked to don the metalic suit of C-3PO, and the diminutive (3'8") Kenny Baker, an actor, pantomime player and cabaret artist who would help to turn R2-D2 from an upside down dustbin into one of the film's most likeable characters.

Also covering up was Bristol-born bodybuilder-turned actor Dave Prowse, familiar from his appearances as the Frankenstein Monster in *Casino Royale* (a gag cameo), *Horror of Frankenstein* and *Frankenstein and the Monster from Hell*. Prowse had also worked for Kubrick, appearing in *A Clockwork Orange*, and his physical stature would add to the presence of Darth Vader, whom he would be playing. (Though at the time of casting, Prowse didn't know that he'd be wearing a mask - or that he would also end up being dubbed by James Earl Jones). Meanwhile, hospital-porter-turned-actor Peter Mayhew got the plum role of Chewbacca. At 7'3", Mayhew was the perfect choice to play the

Peter Cushing in a role he made his own: Vampire hunter extraordinary Van Helsing

Wookiee, and went into *Star Wars* straight from *Sinbad and the Eye of the Tiger*, in which he had been playing a Minotaur.

Back at Industrial Light and Magic (or ILM as everyone was now calling it), progress was being made on the effects - albeit somewhat slowly, given the amount that had to be achieved. Dykstra decided that, to give Lucas the fluidity that was needed in some of the dogfight sequences in the movie, rather than move the models (as had always been the norm) it might be more practical to move the camera, to give the illusion of movement. However, as each effects shot was often made up of various elements (up to forty in some shots), the camera's movement would have to be motion controlled by a computer. It could then recreate exactly a given move over and over again so that each element could be added to the film. All this took time to achieve, as equipment had to be built from scratch. There was no catalogue from which Dykstra and his colleagues could order what they needed.

Ultimately, ILM came up with a gizmo which they dubbed the Dykstraflex System, a piece of hardware able to record moves, each of which could then be repeated ad infinitum. The effects crew also worked on developing optical printers and countless other camera parts. All this cost a lot of money, and soon the Fox accountants were breathing down Dykstra's neck, wanting to know why so much time was being devoted to building all this equipment, while there wasn't anything yet to show for it on film. Nor would there be for some time yet to come. This was a storm Dykstra and his team continually had to ride out. The end results would more than justify the means, however.

Another effects technician working hard prior to the shoot was British make-up artist Stuart Freeborn, whose job it was to realise the film's creatures, among them Chewbacca, the Sand People, the Jawas and the various unsavoury characters found in the Cantina Bar in Mos Eisley. Freeborn had begun his career back in 1936 and had worked on such movies as *The Thief of Baghdad* (one of Lucas's inspirations), *Oliver Twist*, *The Bridge on the River Kwai* (both with Alec Guinness) and *The Omen*. His work for *Star Wars* would help make believable many of Lucas's imaginative concepts. In this task he was assisted by the young Rick Baker, an up-coming make-up artist who would go on to become one of the industry's leading lights, winning Oscars for his work *on An American Werewolf in London, Harry and the Hendersons* (aka *Bigfoot and the Hendersons*), *Ed Wood, The Nutty Professor* and *Men in Black*.

The film's production designer, John Barry, was also hard at work, designing and supervising the building of the huge interior sets needed for the movie at Elstree Studios. Barry also had a team out in Tunisia, building Luke Skywalker's farm and the city of Mos Eisley. The deserts of America, North Africa and the Middle East were all considered before Tunisia was finally settled upon as the location for the planet Tatooine. On the edge of the Sahara, its vast sandy wastes and curious rocky formations provided everything Lucas needed. And it was to Tunisia that Lucas and his cast and crew headed in March 1976. Principal photography was about to commence on March 22nd. There was no turning back now.

8

Playing in the Sand

The dinosaur skeleton seen in the desert of Tatooine was the same skeleton used in Disney's One of our Dinosaurs is Missing.

The Tatooine sequences in Tunisia were filmed near a settlement called Tatahouine.

Following eight weeks of construction, the crew were now ready to start filming. It had been a long struggle just to get this far, and many more obstacles still lay ahead. Nevertheless, *Star Wars* was now beginning to seem a reality.

In the last few weeks leading up to principal photography, Lucas had asked his friends Willard Huyck and Gloria Katz to give his screenplay a quick polish here and there, which they did, mainly concentrating of Leia's dialogue. The story had now finally been locked down...

By no means a futuristic piece, *Star Wars* was set a long time ago in a galaxy far, far away, and centred round the adventures of Luke Skywalker, a farmboy keen to get away from the desert wastes of Tatooine and off to college. His destiny is changed forever, though, when his uncle buys two droids named R2-D2 and C-3PO from a band of Jawas. One of the droids, R2-D2, has had instructions put into his system by Princess Leia, whose Rebel Alliance is battling against the evil Empire. The instructions detail how a giant Death Star can be destroyed, and if the Alliance is to be saved, the information must reach Obi-Wan Kenobi on the planet of Tatooine. Luke agrees to help find Obi-Wan, who he believes to be a hermit called Old Ben. Luke and the robots succeed in finding Obi-Wan, who rescues them from an attack by the Sand People, and the Princess's message is finally delivered.

However, whilst Luke has been away, Imperial Stormtroopers, under the orders of the evil Darth Vader, have killed Luke's aunt and uncle. Now with no home and no family, Luke decides to take up with Ben-Kenobi and the robots, and to help the Rebel Alliance. To do this they make for the Princess's home planet of Alderaan, hiring the services of a maverick pilot, Han Solo, and his Wookiee sidekick, Chewbacca, to take them there in their rundown ship, the Millennium Falcon. Onboard the ship, Luke comes to learn from Obi-Wan the ways of the Jedi Knights, an order of which his late father was a member, and the value of believing in The Force. However, upon reaching Alderaan, the group discovers only a cloud of rubble; Grand Moff Tarkin, commander of the Death Star, has ordered the planet's destruction by an all-powerful tractor beam.

Once through the cloud of rubble, the Millennium Falcon finds itself being pulled inexorably towards the Death Star, which is where Princess Leia is now being held. Luke and Han Solo finally rescue the Princess, whilst Obi-Wan has a run-in with his old enemy, Darth Vader, to whom he sacrifices himself during a light saber fight, so that his comrades might escape. Vader may think he's killed Obi-Wan, but in fact the Jedi Knight has now become a part of The Force itself, guiding Luke from afar.

Having escaped the Death Star in the Millennium Falcon, Luke and his friends join the Rebel Alliance who, from their secret base, launch an attack on the Death Star, successfully destroying it. Chief villain Darth Vader, who has been defending the Death Star during the preceding dog fight, manages to escape to fight another day. Nevertheless, the Alliance is triumphant, and the Princess rewards her heroes in a medal ceremony. It seems all concerned are set to live happily ever after.

The cast and crew that flew off to Tunisia in March was 138 strong, and based themselves at Tozeur in the south of the country. The Tunisian government had actually checked Lucas's script for any subversive political and anti-Moslem references. The military also checked through the company's equipment and props to make sure no weapons were being smuggled in. These formalities completed, they were allowed to go ahead and film, receiving full co-operation from officials.

The first shots Lucas got in the can were at a place called Chotte-el-Djerid, close to Tozur, where he filmed sequences involving the Sand People. Meanwhile, the sandy plains became the farmstead of Luke, his uncle Owen and his aunt Beru, whilst the farm interiors were filmed at the Hotel Sidi Driss in the semi-subterranean town of Matmata. Following the attack of the Stormtroopers in his absence, Luke returns to the homestead to discover the dead bodies of his aunt and uncle, thus spurring him to join Obi-Wan Kenobi. So as to avoid getting a G (for General) certificate, Lucas decided to show Owen and Beru's smouldering remains so as to obtain a PG (Parental Guidance) certificate. The G certificate was associated with harmless Disney comedies, and whilst Lucas was aiming his movie at kids, he didn't want teenagers to dismiss the movie as something intended for eight-year-olds.

Scenes involving robots C-3P0, R2-D2 and the Stormtroopers were filmed on the sand dunes outside Nefta, whilst buildings on the island of Jerba helped form the city of Mos Eisley, at which Skywalker and Obi-Wan Kenobi hire the services of Han Solo. Not everything went smoothly during these first few days, however. The searing heat proved highly uncomfortable for all, especially Alec Guinness in his thick robes and Anthony Daniels sealed inside the fibre-glass casing of C-3PO (which took some two hours to fit). There were also problems with some of the props and mechanical effects.

R2-D2 proved practically impossible for Kenny Baker to operate, and continually fell over. The Jawa's Sandcrawler, built full-size in the desert, was destroyed by desert winds before it could be used. Consequently, the lower portion of the vehicle had to be hastily reconstructed for filming, with the rest to be matted in later. Mechanical effects supervisor John Steers was also put to the test with Luke Skywalker's landspeeder. Supposedly an anti-gravitational vehicle, it was supported for its close-ups by an off-camera rig, which had to support three passengers, a camera and a camera operator, all of which weighed a far from anti-gravitational five tonnes. For long distance shots, the motorized three-wheeler continually broke down. The visible wheels also gave the game away somewhat, and so had to be brushed out by ILM.

But everyone carried on as best they could, despite an outbreak of dysentery and the loss of make-up effects man Stuart Freeborn, who had to be flown back to London when he caught pneumonia. By early April the sequences involving

the Jawas were mostly in the can. Gary Kurtz's young daughters Melissa and Tiffany helped to increase the Jawa population by donning two costumes, as did Kenny Baker's cabaret partner, Jack Purvis, who had been hired along with Baker so as not to unfairly break up the team.

On 2 April, action temporarily came to a halt to celebrate Alec Guinness's sixty-second birthday. Hamill and Guinness were getting on exceptionally well and their scenes together were working as well as Lucas could have hoped for. Other scenes involving Luke were shot, but never made it to the final print, among them a six-minute sequence in which Skywalker joins some friends at a space port to socialize. These scenes (which involved Koo Stark as one of Luke's friends) did appear in the novelization and comic book versions of the story, whilst the scene itself finally turned up on CD-ROM in 1997.

When it came to directing the actors, Lucas didn't say too much on set. This wasn't simply a matter of his innate shyness. He had hired everyone for their personalities - to play an extension of themselves. Though Lucas's lack of character direction was a little awkward for some of the actors to handle, given their lack of experience, the message somehow got across and everyone got on well. The only real personality clash came between Lucas and his cinematographer Gilbert Taylor.

One of Britain's top cameramen Taylor, whose credits took in such important titles as *Seven Days to Noon*, *Ice Cold in Alex* (so he was used to working in the desert), *Dr Strangelove* and *Repulsion*, was one of the few old school technicians working on *Star Wars*, and he quickly made his views on Lucas's more modern approach - which was hands-on in all departments - known. Taylor had actually been Lucas's second choice of cinematographer, his first choice being the legendary Geoffrey Unsworth (*A Night to Remember*, *Northwest Frontier*, *2001*, *Cabaret* and, later, *Superman* and *Tess*). At the last minute, Unsworth decided to pull out of *Star Wars* to go and work with director Vincente Minnelli and his daughter Liza on *A Matter of Time*. A disastrous three-hour epic about a chambermaid who is taught about life by an eccentric countess (Ingrid Bergman), it was finally released (or rather crept out) in a version half its original length, to be greeted by some of the worst reviews ever seen.

In the meantime, Lucas was left with Taylor who, though he contributed enormously to the look of *Star Wars*, only added to Lucas's problems. Lucas

R2-D2 and C-3PO meet the fans

was already behind schedule. Certain scenes that should have been completed in Tunisia had to be abandoned and rescheduled to a later date in California (such as one sequence involving a Bantha, a giant mammoth-like creature), while the company's allotted time in the country was quickly coming to an end. Thus it was with something of a heavy heart that Lucas finally left Tunisia for Elstree, wondering if he'd ever get his vision on screen as intended.

9
England Bound

Luke and Han transfer Chewbacca from cell block 1138.

Harrison Ford's effette impersonation of the guard with the faulty transmitter is a homage to Humphrey Bogart's similar lisping turn in The Big Sleep, *where his Philip Marlowe enters a bookshop in disguise and asks for, 'A Ben-Hur 1860... The one with the erratum on page one-sixteen'.*

If Lucas had hoped that things would improve with his arrival at Elstree, he was sorely mistaken. Like his cameraman Gilbert Taylor, much of the British crew hired to work behind the scenes on *Star Wars* were themselves also entrenched in the old-style, union-led ways of moviemaking. Tea breaks had to be taken on time and the number of hours worked strictly adhered to, whilst each department was responsible for its own props or equipment and no one else's. The fact that the summer of 1976 was one of the hottest on record in Britain only added to the situation. So while Lucas was full of enthusiasm (initially), wanting things to be achieved quickly and to his own specifications, the crew worked by the rule book, even if it meant abandoning a shot towards the end of the day, simply because there wouldn't be enough time to get it in the can before the cast-in-iron knocking off time of 5:30pm. To the crew, *Star Wars* was simply another job.

Some strain also developed between Lucas and Alec Guinness, for during filming Lucas decided that Obi-Wan Kenobi should be killed off during his fight with Darth Vader. Originally, the script had Obi-Wan simply injured, then later rescued by Luke, Han and Leia as they escape the Death Star in the Millennium Falcon. Lucas feared that all this might slow up the action, and so hit upon the idea of having Obi-Wan die and become a guiding spirit - part of the all-powerful Force itself. When Guinness heard about this, he threatened to pull out of the picture. It was only later that he saw the wisdom of Lucas's thinking, especially when he was told that Obi-Wan would continue to be a vocal part of the story in his afterlife.

The studio was also unhappy about Guinness's early death. Guinness was a major star, and to kill him off before the end of the movie seemed like a waste of talent (just as Universal had been up in arms at the fact that Alfred Hitchcock had dared to kill off his star, Janet Leigh, halfway through *Psycho* some sixteen years earlier). The studio wanted Guinness's character to be more involved in the story. But this wasn't *The Alec Guinness Show*, and Obi-Wan was simply one of the many characters the young Luke Skywalker meets on his journey - albeit a highly important one.

Anyone visiting Elstree couldn't fail to be impressed by the huge sets on display and Lucas's command of the technology (if not the crew) needed to get *Star Wars* on screen. Even so, there was not enough space to house all the sets, so the Rebel hangar and the hall for the closing medal ceremony were subsequently built and shot at Shepperton, which at the time had the biggest soundstage in Europe. In fact so big was the Rebel hangar, cardboard cutouts were used for some of the more distant starfighters, so as to save some money on the number of extras needed to fill the place.

One of the most intricate sets, however, proved to be the Millennium Falcon, half of which was built by the on-set art department and supported by a wall concealed behind the craft. Like all the other sets and costumes, it was dirtied down once finished, to give it that all-important lived-in look that Lucas was keen to get across. The X-Wing fighters, meanwhile, weighed in at five tons apiece and took two tower cranes to lift.

Despite Lucas's great attention to detail for the general good of the movie, the attitude of the Fox executives back in Hollywood was to get the film in the can

Ready to ad-lib? A relaxed looking Harrison Ford.

as quickly as possible. Many of them still didn't 'get' *Star Wars* and some of its concepts. They continually asked why the Wookiee didn't wear any clothes, and wanted a line of dialogue inserted to explain the relationship between humans and Jawas instead of letting audiences figure it out for themselves. These were minor considerations, however, given the breakneck speed the film had to be wrapped up in during its last week of shooting. At certain stages, Lucas had three separate crews working on different sequences at the same time, simply to get all the scenes in the can. In order to supervise each unit, Lucas would cycle from set to set.

Lucas wasn't the only person having problems, however. The cast were often up in arms about some of the dialogue they had to speak. Moans about indecipherable technical jargon and the corniness of some of their speeches were a common complaint. Lucas allowed a certain amount of freedom with the script, especially with Harrison Ford, who ad-libbed some good lines along the way. Otherwise, they had to make the best sense they could out of their material. Meanwhile, Carrie Fisher was also having some personal problems. She was insecure about her looks and weight, especially given that she was sent to a health farm prior to shooting to shed ten pounds. Calling herself the Pillsbury Doughgirl, she was convinced that she was going to be replaced throughout the shoot. Lucas's hands-off approach with his cast didn't help matters, either, fuelling Fisher's insecurities. It was at this time that her much-reported problems with drugs apparently began to become more serious, especially during her weekends off, when she would binge on cocaine and LSD.

But as with all nightmare situations, the light at the end of the tunnel eventually grew brighter and shooting at Elstree finally finished in the autumn of 1976. It was no doubt with much relief that Lucas and his wife Marcia packed their bags and left England for home. Yet things were far from over. Not only did the film have to be edited, mixed and scored, there was also the matter of adding the special effects. The question was, would the much-vaunted effects make or break the movie?

10

Post Production

If Tatooine has two suns, then why doesn't everyone and everything have two shadows?

Following a break in Maui, Lucas and his wife Marcia returned to California to begin editing *Star Wars* in earnest at Parkhouse. The first assembley had been far from Lucas's satisfaction, so along with Marcia, Richard Chew and Paul Hirsch, they started the process of putting the movie together from scratch. Editing was not the only hurdle to overcome, though. Of the 365 effects shots required for the movie, just one - that of an escape pod leaving Leia's ship - had been fully completed.

Much of the summer had been spent developing (at a cost of $1m) the equipment needed to achieve the effects, so consequently, little useable footage had been shot. Working conditions had hardly been ideal, either. Temperatures soared in the converted warehouse ILM was housed in, and hours were flexible, many of Dykstra's crew preferring to work at night when things were a little cooler. Lucas was naturally disappointed that so few of the effects had actually been put on film, and so over the next few months split his time between supervising the editing and the effects. Despite everybody's efforts, though, it was soon apparent that the proposed Christmas '76 release date would not be met, and with Fox constantly breathing down his neck, the pressure on Lucas's shoulders became intolerable again - so much so that at one stage he actually spent a few days in hospital for hyper-tension.

Faster and more intense became Lucas's constant cry over the next few months as the effects shots gradually came together. To get things done, a punishing sixteen hour rotation shift was put in place, one shift working from 3pm to mid-night, the other from 8am to 6pm. With each shot costing some $7000, there no time to waste. The shooting of live action footage was by no means over at this stage, however. There were several key moments Lucas had failed to get in the can at either Elstree or in Tunisia. Some sequences also needed re-shooting, among them the Cantina Bar. So, at an added cost of some $100 000, Lucas began filming again.

With the aid of Rick Baker's added make-up effects, extra shots were added to the Cantina Bar to compensate for the fact that Stuart Freeborn had not been able to complete the sequence as intended in Tunisia, owing to his being taken ill with pneumonia. These additions alone cost $20,000 of the $100,000 Lucas had been able to secure from Fox. Meanwhile, at the last minute, stop motion specialists Phil Tippett and Jon Berg were brought in to devise a holographic chess game for Chewbacca and C-3PO to play onboard the Millennium Falcon.

Also outstanding was a sequence featuring the Bantha (a disguised elephant from Marine World), plus several additional shots of Luke's landspeeder, which were completed in Death Valley. Rather than bring back Gilbert Taylor to photograph these pick-ups, Lucas hired Carroll Ballard (later to direct *The Black Stallion*). Unfortunately, Mark Hamill proved unavailable for the work, having been involved in a horrific car crash that had left him minus much of his nose, requiring months of reconstructive plastic surgery using cartilage from his ear. Also required was an aerial view of jungle moon orbiting the planet Yavin, which was filmed by a second unit at the Mayan ruins of Tikal National Park in Guatemala, along with additional close-ups of Greedo, the bounty-hunting alien Solo has a run-in with, and re-shoots of the Jawas carrying R2-D2.

With the help of stricter management practices introduced by Lucas, Kurtz, Jim Nelson and the newly-appointed George Mather, things gradually began to turn around at ILM, and by Christmas 1976 a trailer, accompanied by Holst's *Mars* from the *Planets Suite*, was ready to preview the film. The trailer did much to boost the morale of those working on the movie, though news that it had gone down badly with an audience at the Westwood Cinema, where its tagline 'Coming to your galaxy this summer' was laughed at, threw executive Alan Ladd into a fit of fear. Fox's research team had also come to the conclusion that any movie featuring the word 'war' would put women off going to see it.

Just as ILM were busy working on the visuals for *Star Wars*, so was sound designer Ben Burtt on its aurals. A graduate of USC, Burtt had been working on *Star Wars* practically from the beginning, and whilst Lucas had been filming in Tunisia and London, he had been collecting a wide variety of unconventional sounds to use on the picture. Lucas wanted what he termed an organic soundtrack, and so with this in mind Burtt divided his requirements into various categories: weapons, vehicles, alien voices and doors. These he achieved by recording, then either slowing down or distorting, such sounds as aeroplane engines, animals, domestic appliances and even the Goodyear Blimp. For example, the sound of the light sabres clashing was achieved by hitting the support cable of a radio tower, whilst Chewbacca's vocals were primarily provided by a four-month-old bear called Tarik, recorded by Burtt at San Jose's Happy Hollow Zoo, which he then mixed with walrus, seal and badger noises.

There was also the matter of post-syncronising the sound for sequences in which the original had been unusable, and the dubbing of several characters, most notably that of Darth Vader. Dave Prowse's West Country accent was deemed inappropriate for the role (Carrie Fisher had dubbed him Darth Farmer during filming), so Lucas began looking round for a replacement. An early choice was Orson Welles, at the time popular for his voiceovers for countless TV ads. Ultimately though, Lucas went with Shakespearian actor James Earl Jones, who recorded all of Vader's dialogue in a two-hour session for which he was paid $10 000. His rich baritone voice added immeasurably to Prowse's imposing black-clad figure, though for the original release, Jones didn't receive a credit for his efforts.

Anthony Daniels' vocals also seemed set to be replaced by Lucas, who disliked the actor's English butler-like delivery. The director's original idea had been to give C-3PO a thick Brooklyn accent (though how the robot had acquired this would surely have been hard to justify). Lucas tested thirty people for C-3PO, among them comedian and impersonator Stan Freeberg. Yet whilst continually watching and listening to Daniels' performance during these dubbing sessions, Lucas gradually came to realise that the two were inseparable. Daniels' original dialogue had been recorded using a tiny microphone tucked into the left eyebrow of the robot's mask. Naturally, this

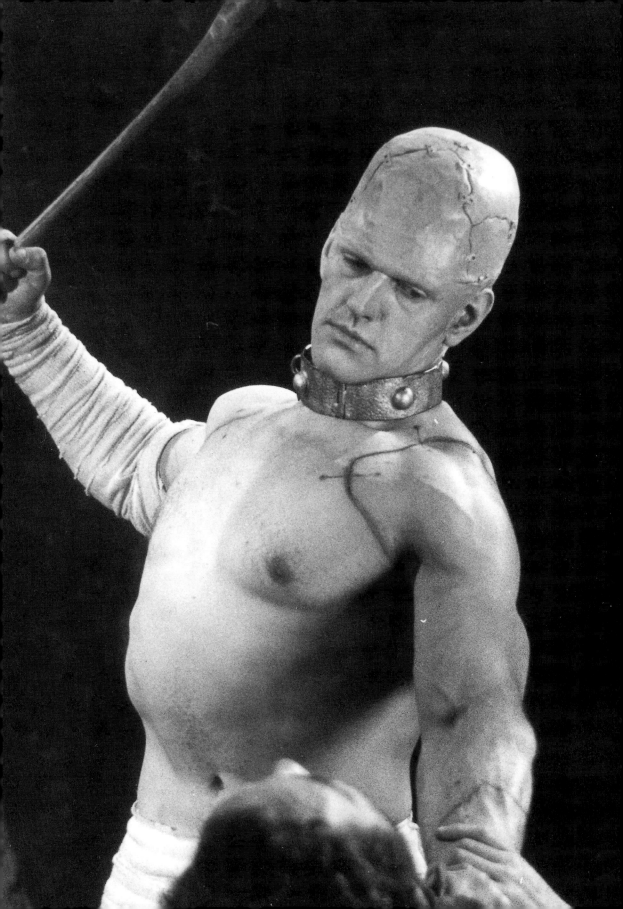

also picked up Daniels' breathing, the movement of the costume and its frequent banging into things. Nevertheless, despite these distractions, the character came over, and so Lucas decided to keep Daniels' vocal after all, and so invited the actor out to LA to dub it.

With the film slowly nearing completion, the question of marketing and merchandising now became a priority for Fox in early 1977. The studio's advertising chief David Weitzner thus hired the successful advertising firm of Smolen, Smith and Connolly to take on the task. The company had successfully launched *Carrie* for United Artists and *The Omen* for Fox the previous year, and were currently also working on the campaign for Woody Allen's *Annie Hall* (also for United Artists). In turn, they brought in Tom Jung to develop initial poster concepts for the movie. Having watched a rough cut, Jung decided to base his designs round the film's basic premise of good versus evil, producing a poster featuring a somewhat muscular Luke Skywalker holding up a light saber in front of a blow-up of Darth Vader's black mask. Meanwhile, in front of Luke, Princess Leia - hand on hip, flashing her legs - takes on a somewhat sultry-looking Bond girl pose. The poster also features R2-D2, C-3PO, the Death Star, a squadron of TIE fighters and the tag line, 'A long time ago in a galaxy far, far away...'.

There had already been a teaser poster, released in late 1976, which had featured the soon-to-be-famous *Star Wars* logo. There would also be other poster designs by other artists as the movie's launch date neared, yet it was Jung's poster that launched the main press campaign, appearing in national press ads in New York and Los Angeles on Sunday 15 May. This poster, subsequently re-worked at George Lucas's request by Tim and Gregg Hildebrandt to have a more comic book feel to it, re-appeared the following weekend and thereafter would remain an integral part of the advertising campaign.

Whilst the advertising campaign was gaining momentum, things were still pretty slow to take off regarding the merchandising. Despite the best efforts of Charlie Lippincott, toy manufacturers just weren't interested in *Star Wars*. Both Mattel and Ideal turned down the opportunity to manufacture *Star Wars* toys, much to their eventual cost. Eventually, a deal was secured with Kenner, though even they proved less than enthusiastic. Where Lippincott did gain ground,

The man behind Darth Vader's mask. Dave Prowse in action as the Monster in Hammer's *Horror of Frankenstein* however, was at the various science fiction conventions up and down the country, which he, Kurtz and, until his accident, Mark Hamill visited, taking with them artwork, storyboards and models used in the film. The heads of toy companies may have been immune to the charms of *Star Wars*, yet at the grass roots level, fans were beginning to take an interest. In fact, the novelization of the *Star Wars* screenplay by Allan Dean Foster, which had been published by Del Ray in November 1976, had sold its initial 100,000 copy print run by February. The Marvel *Star Wars* comic was also flying off the newsstands at a gratifying rate.

Yet apart from Alan Ladd, Fox remained convinced that *Star Wars* was not going to be the event Lucas was expecting it to be, nor the increasing ground swell was indicating it would be. In fact for the executives, the studio's romantic weepie *The Other Side of Midnight*, based on the Sidney Sheldon novel, was surely going to be the big hit of the summer as far as they were concerned. Cinema owners were also proving reluctant to book the film, and had it not been for the delayed release of Universal's *Sorceror* (a big budget, hyped-up remake *of The Wages of Fear* that quickly disappeared when it finally appeared), *Star Wars* wouldn't even have managed a booking at the showcase Grauman's Chinese Theatre on Hollywood Boulevard.

Meanwhile, post-production was grinding on. John Williams had by now been hired to score the movie, having been introduced to Lucas by his friend Steven Spielberg, for whom Williams had scored *The Sugarland Express* and *Jaws*. Though he is now recognized as the pre-eminent film composer of his generation, at the time Williams' career was just beginning to skyrocket.

Born in 1932, Williams began studying to be a concert pianist at the age of sixteen under the tutelage of Bobby Van Epps. In 1951, Williams joined the US Air Force, and over the next three years orchestrated and conducted service bands. Once he left the Air Force, Williams continued his studies at the Juilliard School of Music and, later, UCLA. In 1956 he entered films as a studio pianist, first for Columbia, then for Fox. Then, in the late fifties following further experience as an orchestrator, Williams began composing for television, among his early credits being episodes of *Wagon Train*. He also broke into film scoring in 1959 with *Daddy-O*. Further film and television assignments followed, among them *Because They're Young, I Passed for White, Checkmate* (his first TV title theme) and *Gilligan's Island*.

By the late sixties, Williams had several memorable TV themes to his credit, among them *Lost in Space* and *Land of the Giants*. However, though he'd scored several popular comedies such as *Penelope* and *Fitzwilly*, and had earned Oscar nominations for his musical direction on *Valley of the Dolls* and *Goodbye, Mr Chips*, it wasn't until he scored *The Reivers* in 1969 and earned another Oscar nomination that studios began to take note of his talents. Following his first Oscar win for his adaptation of *Fiddler on the Roof* in 1971, Williams hit a lucky streak, scoring such successes as *The Cowboys*, *The Poseidon Adventure*, *Earthquake*, *The Towering Inferno* and *The Eiger Sanction*. It was his ominous score for *Jaws*, however, that would put him on the map and win him a best score Oscar, thanks to his thumping shark theme.

Williams' music for *Star Wars* would be the icing on Lucas's creation. However, Lucas at first wanted the composer to adapt established classical pieces for the movie, rather like Stanley Kubrick had done with *2001*. Indeed, Lucas had already overlaid music from Holst's *The Planets Suite* and Miklos Rozsa's *Ben-Hur* score to the rough cut. Williams wasn't too keen on this idea though, preferring to write something new for the movie, taking his inspiration from the lavish swashbuckling scores of Erich Wolfgang Korngold, giving each character their own identifiable *leitmotif*.

Lucas was delighted with the various themes Williams came up with and gave him the go-ahead to compose the full score. Ultimately, Williams would write 88 minutes of original music for *Star Wars* (the running time of which would finally come in at 121 minutes). This was in turn orchestrated by Williams' regular assistant Herbert W. Spencer, and recorded by the 87-piece London Symphony Orchestra at the Anvil Studios at Denham between 5 March and 16 March. Lucas flew back to Britain to produce the sessions himself, which were recorded by Eric Tomlinson and supervised by Fox's head of music, Lionel Newman. Ironically, it was Newman's elder brother Alfred (in whose orchestra Williams had played in the fifties) who had composed the studio's well-known *Fox Fanfare*, which Williams also re-recorded during the *Star Wars* sessions, giving it a Dolby Stereo make-over.

The release date was now set for 25 May, and the race was on to get the movie completed in time. This involved the mixing of the music, some final editing tweaks and the insertion of some effects shots still outstanding. In paring the movie down to as near to two hours as Lucas could get it, there were inevitably some cutting room floor casualties. Some of the sequences on Tatooine were trimmed, while the early scenes between Luke and his buddy Biggs Darklighter, played by Garrick Hagon, were cut completely. This left only only Luke's encounter with Biggs towards the end of the movie at the Rebel

base (which explains why they're otherwise unaccountably so glad to see each other).

Another sequence involving Han Solo's run-in with Jabba the Hutt, to whom he owes money, was also cut in its entirety. In this brief scene, Jabba was played by Irish actor Declan Mullholland, who had pipped William Hootkins to the role (Hootkins instead played Rebel pilot Porkins). Jabba of course eventually re-appeared again in *Return of the Jedi*, this time as a giant slug-like creature, which meant that when Lucas restored the scene for the 1997 anniversary re-release, it had to be adjusted (with computer generated effects) to show the character audiences were familiar with. Which meant Mullholland's performance ended up on the cutting room floor a second time!

Still, the Fox executives remained unimpressed by the movie - perhaps because the effects weren't quite completed - so to cover these gaps Lucas had padded out the footage with clips from a number of World War Two movies! Thus Lucas arranged a screening for some of his movie friends to gain some feedback. Among those invited were Steven Spielberg, Brian de Palma, William Huyck, Gloria Katz, John Milius, Hal Barwood, Matthew Robbins and Jay Cocks, a writer with *Time* magazine. Apart from Cocks and Spielberg (who predicted the movie would make over $100m), all were unimpressed by Lucas's labours. De Palma was particularly critical, yet this didn't prevent Lucas from accepting his and Cocks's offer to re-write the movie's opening explanatory scrawl which was originally almost three times longer than it is now.

If Lucas had been disappointed by the reaction of his friends, he took solace in the fact that a test screening on 30 April went down a storm at San Francisco's North Point Theatre. By this time Williams's score was in place and the effects fully completed. The audience loved the movie. A number of press screenings were also held in May. The opening date was now approaching fast. America was about to get its first taste of the *Star Wars* phenomenon.

Left on the cutting room floor: Declan Mulholland, the unseen Jabba the Hutt

11

The Force is With Him

Darth Vader is Dutch for dark father.

Right up to the last possible moment, Lucas worked away on *Star Wars*, tinkering here, tightening there. So much so that prints of the film's last reel arrived at some cinemas after the first 10am screenings had begun.

Despite the lack of a huge publicity drive, plus the fact that the movie was opening on a Wednesday instead of a Friday or Saturday, queues for *Star Wars* began forming at cinemas at 8am - some two hours before the first show. A phenomenon - not even seen with the likes of *Jaws*, *The Godfather* or *The Exorcist* - was beginning to take hold, with audiences staying in their seats to see the movie a second or even third time. Naturally, this caused problems for theatre managers, who quickly had to revise their standing policy which allowed audience members to enter the cinema when they chose, and leave when they chose. If only to deal with the huge crowds waiting to get in, cinemas now had to be cleared between each showing of *Star Wars*.

Lucas spent most of that opening Wednesday mixing a special six track sound print of *Star Wars* (to play in LA and New York), and so remained unaware of what was happening with his movie. It was only in the evening, when he and Marcia decided to go out for dinner to their favourite hamburger restaurant, The Hamburger Hamlet (which just happened to be across the street from Grauman's Chinese Theatre) that it gradually dawned on the couple that *Star Wars* was a smash.

In fact on its opening day the movie brought in $254,309, which was quite remarkable given that it was only playing at a scant 32 cinemas in major cities across America (another nine would quickly be added at the weekend). Competition on that opening day wasn't too strong, comprising of such duds as *The Deep* and *Exorcist II: The Heretic*. Nevertheless, those audience members who couldn't get in to see *Star Wars* (over 5000 at one cinema!) were instead going to see their second or third choice of movie, preferring to return at a later date to catch up with *Star Wars*. This had the unforseen effect of boosting the box office takes of other movies!

House records were being broken at all the cinemas playing *Star Wars*. As a consequence, shares in Fox, which had been an unimpressive $11 before the movie opened, shot to $21 the following Monday. Bemused executives who had written the film off were now hailing Lucas, Kurtz and Alan Ladd as geniuses! Meanwhile, on the street, positive word of mouth about the movie was spreading like wildfire. Even the press, whose critics could have put a damper on things, fell in love with the movie. Fox couldn't have bought better reviews.

'Lucas and producer Gary Kurtz [have] assembled an enormous technical crew, drawn from the entire Hollywood production pool of talent, and the results equal the genius of Walt Disney, Willis O'Brien and other justifiably famous practitioners of what Irwin Allen calls movie magic,' enthused *Variety*, which then went on to praise the cast. 'Carrie Fisher is delightful as the regal but spunky princess who has been kidnapped by Peter Cushing, would-be ruler of the universe. Mark Hamill, previously a TV player, is excellent as a farm boy who sets out to rescue Fisher in league with Alec Guinness, last survivor of a band of noble knights. Harrison Ford is outstanding as a likeable mercenary pilot.'

The *Hollywood Reporter* also liked the film, commenting, '*Star Wars* will undoubtedly emerge as one of the true classics in the genre of science fiction/fantasy films. In any event, it will be thrilling audiences of all ages for a long time to come.' An uncannily accurate prediction. 'Pure sweet fun all the

Darth Vader meets an adoring public

way' added *Newsweek*, while *The New York Times* described the film as 'A mind-blowing spectacle that sends the audience off into the wondrously strange world of fantasy and satisfies just about everyone's adolescent craving for a corny old-fashioned adventure movie.' Charles Champlin called *Star Wars*, 'The year's most razzle-dazzling family movie, an exuberant and technically astonishing space adventure' concluding that it was, 'Buck Rogers with a doctoral degree.'

There were some dissenters. 'It's all trite characters and paltry verbiage', moaned John Simon, to which the usually astute Pauline Kael added, 'You may feel cheated of some dimension - a sense of wonder, perhaps.' Their views were in the minority, though.

In fact the surprise success of the opening of *Star Wars* quickly became a news item in itself. 'There was only one topic of conversation in the film industry yesterday - the smash opening of George Lucas's *Star Wars*,' reported *Variety* on the Thursday. Indeed, the block long queues outside cinemas made the evening news. Everyone was talking about *Star Wars*. Everyone, that is, except Lucas and his wife who, the day after the opening, took off for a pre-planned trip to Maui. At the most important point of his career, the man of the moment was nowhere to be found. Instead, he and Marcia were re-charging their batteries with a much-needed break. Even with his feet up, though, Lucas couldn't stop thinking about future projects and, bumping into his friend Steven Spielberg on the vacation (himself recovering from the production traumas of *Close Encounters*), he outlined an idea he had about the adventures of an archaeologist...

But that was in the future. On his return home, Lucas had to contend with the sudden interest in *Star Wars*. Publishing houses and toy companies were now falling over each other to secure the rights to sell *Star Wars* merchandise, something which must surely have given Lucas a great sense of satisfaction.

As interest in the movie continued to mount, Lucas hired Charles Weber to help field the merchandising offers, his criteria being quality rather than the best financial deal. Consequently, spacecraft models, character figurines, masks, cookies (Wookiee cookies), souvenir programmes, posters, tee-shirts, pinball machines, underwear, pillow cases and lunch boxes began to appear over the next few months. In fact by Christmas 1978, Kenner had managed to sell an incredible 42 million character figurines. Also proving popular was Allan Dean Foster's novelization which was still continueing to sell well (it quickly reached the bestseller lists), whilst Marvel were soon on their third print run of the first three issues of the comic books.

Even John Williams' double-LP symphonic soundtrack record - not the kind of music to usually sell in vast amounts to your average cinemagoer - went on to become the number one soundtrack album of all time, selling some one million copies in America alone, making an incredible $16m for Fox's record division, which had of course been reluctant to release it. Meanwhile, a disco version of Williams' main theme by Meco Monardo hit the number one spot in the US Billboard chart in October '77, where it remained for two weeks. In fact Monardo's accompanying album, *Star Wars and Other Galactic Funk*, outsold Williams's original, producing a showdown at the following year's Grammy

Awards, when both Monardo and Williams were nominated in the best instrumental category (which Williams won).

As the money kept rolling in, Lucas rewarded his stars, awarding Hamill, Ford and Fisher two percentage points in the movie, which turned into $650,000 each. Kurtz was on five per cent of the net profits, whilst William Huyck and Gloria Katz were on two. John Williams, ILM's Jim Nelson and Lucas's lawyer Tom Pollack were also awarded points. In all, Lucas gave a cash bonus to eighteen people, including Ralph McQuarrie and model designer Joe Johnston, who received a percentage of the vast merchandising profits. Lucas could afford it, for at the end of its first run, *Star Wars* had grossed $232m in America, the highest box-office figure to that date. Worldwide, the take was $430m, plus another $3 billion in profits from merchandising (Kenner ultimately made $7 billion from its *Star Wars* lines of merchandising).

The movie was, by early 1978, a global event, whether it was *Stjarnornas Krig* (in Sweden), *Sterne Krigen* (Norway), *Guerra Stellari* (Italy), *La Guerra de las Galaxias* (Spain), *Krieg Der Sterne* (Germany), *Stjernekrigen* (Denmark) or *La Guerres des Etoiles* (France). Indeed, so well known had the film's characters become - and so quickly - Ted Mann, the owner of Grauman's Chinese Theatre, invited C-3PO, R2-D2 and Darth Vader to make their footprints in cement in the theatre's hall of fame forecourt. Naturally, the event, attended by thousands of fans, was a major accolade for Lucas, and garnered even more positive publicity for the movie, making print and television news across America.

In 1978, *Star Wars* finally came to Britain, premiering at London's Dominion Theatre in January, though performances were actually sold out until March. As it had in America, *Star Wars* mania swept the country, with British fans proving equally voiciferous in their enthusiasm for the film. Again, the press was also mostly enthusiastic. 'The all-time inter-galactic money spinner', said *The News of the World*, to which *The Daily Express* added, 'This film is visually astonishing, exciting and, most of all, fun.' Audiences couldn't agree more and, as in the USA, queued to see it again and again.

Meanwhile, back in America, the Academy Award nomination had been announced, and *Star Wars* had received a healthy ten nominations. They were for best picture, best director (Lucas), best screenplay (Lucas), best supporting actor (Alec Guinness), best editing (Marcia Lucas, Paul Hirsch, Richard Chew), best score (John Williams), best art direction and set decoration (John Barry, Norman Reynolds, Leslie Dilley, Roger Christian), best costume design (John

Mollo), best sound (Don MacDougal, Ray West, Bob Minkler, Derek Ball) and best visual effects (John Dykstra, John Stears, Richard Edlund, Grant McCune, Robert Blalack). The film won six of these award (editing, score, art direction, costume, sound and effects), plus a special achievement award for Ben Burtt's sound effects. It also won a Class II plaque for Scientific or Technical Achievement.

While his wife Marcia walked away with her own golden statuette, Lucas personally failed to win a single award. Best picture went to *Annie Hall* (with *The Goodbye Girl*, *Julia* and *The Turning Point* also losing out), whilst Woody Allen and Marshall Brickman won for best screenplay for *Annie Hall*, as did Allen for best director. Alec Guinness meanwhile lost the supporting actor gong to Jason Robards, who won for *Julia*.

The Oscars were by no means the only awards *Star Wars* were in line for. The movie also won two Los Angeles Film Critics' Awards (best film and score), one Golden Globe (best score), a BAFTA (best score) and an incredible thirteen Science Fiction, Horror and Fantasy Film Awards.

Not all was glitz and glory, however. The film's stars often found it hard to deal with fame on such an instant and gigantic level. Personal appearances to promote the movie were met with scenes of hysteria akin to those that greeted The Beatles in the 1960s. This put an incredible strain on private lives, to such a degree that Fisher came to rely more and more on drugs to deal with the situation, whilst Ford found his marriage collapsing. Lucas also hated all the attention, so withdrew to The Parkhouse, leaving only when business required that he do so. The continuous uphill battle to make the movie had left Lucas shattered too. So much so that he vowed never to direct a movie again (it would be over twenty years before he would do so).

As the months rolled by, the *Star Wars* phenomenon showed no sighs of abating. A year to the day after its release, a special first birthday poster was issued to cinemas still playing the film. Showing a giant birthday cake surrounded by a selection of the Kenner character figurines, its tag line read, 'May the Force be with You - One Year Old Today.' Then, in the summer of 1978, the movie was re-released, taking a further $46m at the box office. By this time, the movie had a new title: *Star Wars, Episode IV: A New Hope*. Lucas explained that the movie was the opening story in a central trilogy that would ultimately run to nine episodes, the next episode of which would be *Chapter V*. As *The Hollywood Reporter* had rightly predicted, *Star Wars* would be thrilling audiences of all ages for a long time to come.

12
After Effects

In More American Graffiti, *Harrison Ford makes an uncredited cameo appearance as Bob Falfa, who has now become a traffic cop.*

As Lucas took a deserved break from the *Star Wars* universe, everyone else attempted to emulate its success. As a movie genre, science fiction had been resuscitated overnight, and other studios were keen to get on the bandwagon. Among those attempting to emulate the success of *Star Wars* were Disney (with *Tron*, *The Spaceman and King Arthur*, *The Cat from Outer Space* and *The Black Hole*), Paramount (*Star Trek*, plus re-releases of *When Worlds Collide* and *War of the Worlds*), Warner Bros.. (*Superman*), New World (*Battle Beyond the Stars*), EMI (*Flash Gordon*), United Artists (*Moonraker*) and ITC (*Saturn Three*). Even Fox continued to look to the skies with *Alien*, which proved a commercial success, as did Columbia's *Close Encounters of the Third Kind*, which had been directed by Lucas's buddy Steven Spielberg and released the same year. There were also plenty of cheap imitations, among them *Starcrash*, *The Shape of Things to Come*, *The Humanoid* and *Starship Invasions*. Even television got in on the act, developing *Buck Rogers in the 25th Century* and, most notably, *Battlestar Galactica*.

John Dykstra's Cylon warriors from *Battlestar Galactica*
could be cousins to *Star Wars*' Imperial Stormtroopers

Of all the films and programmes made to cash in on the *Star Wars* phenomenon, it was *Battlestar Galactica*, made by Universal, that caught Lucas's eye the most, for it contained effects by none other than John Dykstra. Dykstra also helped to produce the show with its creator Glen Larson (who would later be behind the *Buck Rogers* revival). There had been little love lost between Lucas and Dykstra during the effects shoot for *Star Wars*, and after the movie was finished Dykstra left ILM to create his own effects company, Apogee, which he at first housed in the same Van Nuys warehouse, renting it from Fox. Several other effects technicians from ILM (which had since been relocated to San Rafael) remained with Dykstra, much to Lucas's chagrin.

73

The first episode of *Battlestar Galactica* aired on 23 June 1978 and was an instant hit. Feeling his ideas for *Star Wars* had been ripped off for the series, Lucas urged Fox to take Universal to court over the programme. Universal counter-sued, claiming that Lucas had ripped off ideas from *their* 1971 sci-fi movie *Silent Running*. The various cases took almost three years to be resolved, the final judgement declaring that all the parties involved had, to some extent, been guilty of infringement. This must have irked Lucas somewhat, given the success of *Battlestar Galactica*, several episodes of which were also edited together to make a theatrical feature. Some fans even confused *Galactica* with *Star Wars*, believing Lucas to be the man behind both projects.

Fans keen for a sequel to the real thing were not to be disappointed, though, for by the time *Battlestar Galactica* hit the airwaves, Lucas had already announced to his intention to produce (though not direct) a sequel to *Star Wars*. Before this appeared, though, there was the matter of an outstanding contract obligation with Universal to fulfil. Under the terms of his *American Graffiti* contract, Lucas owed the studio another film, which he decided would be a sequel to his 1973 hit to be called *More American Graffiti*.

Lucas worked mainly in a supervisory capacity on the film, acting as its executive producer. The producer's chores he handed over to to Howard Kazanjian (his USC classmate, who by now had worked on the likes of *The Wild Bunch* and *Rollercoaster*), whilst to write and direct the movie he brought in William Lloyd Norton, then known primarily for a 1971 drugs movie called *Cisco Pike*, which had starred Gene Hackman, Kris Kristofferson, Karen Black and Harry Dean Stanton. He had also scripted *Convoy* for Sam Peckinpah.

Norton based his script on ideas by himself, Lucas and Kazanjian. Originally titled *Purple Haze* (but later re-titled by Universal in a bid to be more commercial), it brought back many of the characters from the original. Among them were Steve and Laurie (who are now expecting a baby), Terry the Toad (who is about to be shipped off to Vietnam), John (who is now a hotrod racer) and Debbie (who is living with a guitar player). As well as Vietnam, the movie, set between 1964 and 1967, also took in campus riots and flower power.

Save for Richard Dreyfus, all the cast returned to reprise their roles, including Ron Howard (who had been enjoying great success on television in the *American Graffiti*-insipred sit-com *Happy Days*), Paul LeMat, Cindy Williams, Candy Clark, Charles Martin Smith and Mackenzie Phillips, whilst Wolfman Jack could again be heard over the airwaves. Even Harrison Ford re-appeared briefly, uncredited, as Bob Falfa, who is now a motorcycle cop.

The narrative's multiple storylines unfolded in an almost experimental non-linear fashion, with Norton making use of split-screen at certain points. Yet despite some strong sequences in Vietnam and during anti-war riots, all slickly photographed by Caleb Deschanel, Norton wasn't entirely comfortable with the film's structure, and audiences were similarly turned off by the movie's approach, despite another soundtrack rich with sixties pop and rock.

'More American Graffiti may be one of the most innovative and ambitious films of the last five years, but by no means is it one of the most successful', commented Variety, going on to say, 'In trying to follow the success of George Lucas's immensely popular 1973 hit, writer-director B.W.L. Norton overloads the sequel with four wholly different cinematic styles to carry forward the lives of American Graffiti's original cast.'

Well worth seeking out for the curious, More American Graffiti, though a box office failure, does nevertheless contain many interesting sequences, given that it was Lucas's first post Star Wars production. Arguably ahead of its time, the movie is perhaps ready for re-evaluation.

Lucas wasn't the only person not having success with their post Star Wars projects. Aside from a few appearances on Saturday Night Live, Carrie Fisher's career was failing to take off, her only movie between Star Wars and its sequel being Mr Mikes Mondo Video, a pseudo-mondo movie shot on video for television. Made by and involving many of the talents associated with Saturday Night Live, among them comics Dan Aykroyd, Bill Murray and Gilda Radner, it was refused an airing by NBC, and so was instead picked up for a (limited) theatrical release by Roger Corman's New Line company. It was certainly a comedown from Star Wars.

Mark Hamill's career also curiously failed to skyrocket, though he certainly did better than Mr Mike's Mondo Video with Corvette Summer (aka The Hot One), a fairly cheerful comedy in which he played a student who spends his summer vacation looking for his stolen Corvette. Written by Lucas's USC buddies Hal Barwood and Matthew Robbins (with Barwood also producing and Robbins directing), the movie is likeable enough, but failed to set the box office alight. Neither did the much better Big Red One, an excellent war movie written and directed by the veteran Samuel Fuller, in which Hamill co-starred with Lee Marvin and Robert Carradine.

Though he would ultimately become a superstar (he would be voted Star of the Century in 1994 by American exhibitors), Harrison Ford's career between Star Wars and its follow up, though busy, was certainly nothing to write home about either. He made a brief appearance in Francis Ford Coppola's *Apocalypse Now*, in which he played Colonel G. Lucas! He also starred in two movies set during World War Two: *Hanover Street*, a romantic drama co-starring Lesley-Anne Down and Christopher Plummer which he shot in London, and *Force Ten from Navarone*, an actioner with Robert Shaw, Franco Nero, Barbara Bach, Edward Fox and Richard Kiel. There was also a disappointing comedy, *The Frisco Kid*, which partnered Ford with Gene Wilder to little effect.

To keep fans happy before the emergence of the *Star Wars* sequel, Lucas okayed a TV special, which was aired on CBS on 17 November 1978. Called *The Star Wars Holiday Extravaganza*, it received just one broadcast owing to the poor quality of its content. Opening with stock footage of Han Solo and Chewbacca fleeing from two Imperial Cruisers, the programme then went into an opening title sequence declaring that it starred Jefferson Starship, Diahann Carroll and Beatrice Arthur (now best known for her role in the classic TV sit-com *The Golden Girls*). As things unfold, we visit Chewbacca's home planet and meet his wife Mala, his child Lumpy and his father Itchy.

A painful experience, the programme contains brief appearances by Mark Hamill, who is seen on a video screen; Harrison Ford, who visits his Wookiee pal's family; and Carrie Fisher, who gets to sing a song based on the *Star Wars* theme. Meanwhile, Bea Arthur leads a group of drunken aliens in a sing-along in the Cantina Bar in Mos Eisley, while Itchy watches Diahann Carroll singing seventies hits on TV (eh?). As bad as all this is, in recent years *Star Wars* devotees have demanded to see the programme again out of sheer curiosity value. However, at a later convention, Lucas reportedly told an audience that if he had a hammer and the time, he would track down all the existing copies of the programme and destroy them. This was one item that obviously slipped through the otherwise vigorous vetting process of Lucasfilm's licensing division! That said, another sanctioned programme already aired, which told the story of the making of *Star Wars*, as hosted by C-3PO and R2-D2, was also pretty squirm-making.

What fans wanted was more of the real thing. In 1980, they finally got it in the shape of *The Empire Strikes Back*. And though he didn't direct the movie, this time Lucas was definitely calling the shots.

13
Empire Building

Jeremy Bulloch, who plays Boba Fett, also makes an uncredited cameo appearance as an Imperial Commander in Cloud City.

A reference is made by General Rieekan to 'rogues ten and eleven, station three-eight'(ie: 1138).

Just as he had done on *More American Graffiti*, Lucas delegated the roles of writer and director to others on *The Empire Strikes Back*. But as the film's executive producer and the author of its story, there was no doubt as to who was in charge.

Again, Lucas and his lawyer Tom Pollack brokered an astonishing deal for *The Empire Strikes Back*. Given that he owned the rights to all sequels, as cannily stated in his original *Star Wars* contract, Fox therefore need not necessarily be the studio through which Lucas would release *Empire*! Using this as a bargaining chip with Fox who, much to their chagrin, had to negotiate the rights to distribute the movie, Lucas more or less dictated his contract to the studio.

Basically, it involved him financing the $18m cost of the movie himself through Lucasfilm, by mortgaging profits from *Star Wars* (it was always his intention to re-invest his money into the industry). This meant all of *Empire's* profits would go to Lucas and Lucasfilm. Fox would just get a distributor's fee which, even if the film did just half as well as *Star Wars*, would still be substantial. There was also the kudos of being associated with the most successful franchise in film history. This came at a price, though. There would be no studio interference on *Empire* as there had been on *Star Wars*. All Fox knew was that the movie would have a 1980 release!

Of course, all this was an incredible gamble on Lucas's part. If *Star Wars* proved to be a one shot wonder, then Lucas would lose everything if *Empire* flopped. However, if it was the hit he was hoping for, his dream of building his own studio complex away from Hollywood would move closer to reality. Lucas had already spent some of his *Star Wars* cash on acquiring land in San Rafael where one day he hoped to build a $20m complex of editing suites and recording studios. Yet as *Empire* went into production, all of this was far from being the dead cert hindsight has since proved it to have been.

Fox wasn't the only company whose feathers were ruffled by Lucas's Empire deal. His agency, ICM, were also miffed that Lucas and Pollack had done all the negotiating themselves instead of involving the agency, as had been the case on *Star Wars*. Because they had helped to broker the *Star Wars* deal, ICM had consequently earned ten percent of Lucas's gross earnings on the film. Lucas didn't see why he needed to use ICM's services this time round, given the massive bargaining power he now had. ICM disagreed and took Lucas to court. They failed in their case, however, the judgement stating that Lucas had every right to negotiate his own deal. Consequently, ICM didn't make a penny from *Empire*. In the process, they also lost one of their most valuable clients, which had the immediate effect of devaluing the company's shares.

The official announcement that there would be a sequel to *Star Wars* was originally made on 24 February 1978, though it wasn't until 4 August of the same year that the title was finally confirmed. The idea for the title came from the film's producer Gary Kurtz, and had come about when he'd been asked in a publicity interview for *Star Wars* what he thought a sequel might be called. Given the serial-like nature of *Star Wars*, Kurtz jokingly suggested that it might be something like *The Empire Strikes Back*. The joke stuck, however, and, out of all the potential titles considered, it proved to be the one that worked best.

By now Lucas was working on a scene by scene treatment of the film's story, based on his original epic *Star Wars* script. He didn't want to write the script itself, though, so handed his notes to veteran screenwriter Leigh Brackett. Known for her smart dialogue, Brackett had scripted many movies for director Howard Hawks, among them *The Big Sleep*, *Rio Bravo*, *Rio Lobo*, *Hatari* and *El Dorado*. More importantly, she was also a noted science fiction writer, having penned such books as *The Sword of Rhiannon*, *The Ginger Star*, *The Long Tomorrow* and *The Starmen of Llyrdis*.

Following Lucas's scene plan, Brackett wrote a three act script which opened on the ice planet of Hoth where the Rebel Alliance, led by Luke Skywalker, Princess Leia and Han Solo, are now based. When their whereabouts is discovered by Darth Vader, a huge battle with the Imperial forces follows. Having won the battle, though not necessarily the war, Luke is then sent by the ghostly Obi-Wan Kenobi to the swamp planet of Dagobah, where he is to be taught the mystical ways of the Jedi by the ancient Yoda. This accomplished, Skywalker would then travel to the sky city above the planet Bespin, where Solo and Leia are being held by Vader. In confronting Vader, Luke gets a nasty surprise, for it turns out that Vader is his father...

In her writing, Brackett gave some of the dialogue, particularly the exchanges between Skywalker, Solo and Leia, a sharp wisecracking thirties quality. She also helped to round and develop all the key characters, making them more three-dimensional. When she finished this preliminary draft, she sent it to Lucas, who was pleased with her efforts. He then expected Brackett to continue working on the script through several more drafts. Sadly, Brackett had been keeping a secret. She was dying from cancer, and passed away just days after sending her script to Lucas. She was sixty-three.

This obviously came as something of a blow to Lucas and Kurtz. Nevertheless, Lucas took over the script himself for a period, working on it whilst holidaying in Mexico with Marcia and his friend director Michael Ritchie and his wife. Lucas then handed this draft to up-coming screenwriter Lawrence Kasdan, who was developing Lucas's idea for a film about the adventures of an archaeologist at the time. A former copy writer, Kasdan had only just turned to screenwriting with *Continental Divide*, a thirties-style romantic comedy which was to be directed by Michael Apted, with John Belushi and Blair Brown taking the leads. The film was to be made by Spielberg's Amblin company through Universal, and it was Spielberg who introduced Kasdan to Lucas. Of course Kasdan would go on to write and direct such modern classics as *Body Heat*, *The Big Chill* and *The Accidental Tourist*. At this stage in his burgeoning career, however, he was happy to be working on such high profile projects, to which he brought a greater emotional texture than normally found in such fare.

Meanwhile, as the script was progressing, there was the matter of who would actually direct *The Empire Strikes Back*. Gary Kurtz compiled a list of some one hundred directors, which Lucas then whittled down to twenty. Whoever was chosen, Lucas said, had to balance the film's effects with drama and character. For a while rumour had it that Steven Spielberg would helm *Empire*. The eventual choice was somewhat surprising, with Lucas deciding upon Irvin Kershner.

Lucas and Kurtz of course knew Kershner from his days as a teacher at USC. Born in 1923, he was considerably older than the producer and director. A violin prodigy, Kershner had first turned to painting, sculpting and photography as a career before starting to teach photography at USC in 1949. In 1958 he turned to film, directing the hard-boiled drugs drama *Stakeout on Dope Street*, which he followed with such eclectic fare as *The Hoodlum Priest*, *A Fine Madness*, *Loving* and *The Eyes of Laura Mars*. Nothing, really, to indicate that he might be suitable to take on a big budget action adventure. What he did have in his favour, however, was his fine work with actors, plus the fact that he worked quickly and efficiently.

Kershner also had his doubts about taking on *Empire*, though. If *Star Wars* had in fact been a one shot wonder, he didn't want to be the person to bankrupt Lucas. He was also concerned that critics would be continually comparing his direction of the movie to Lucas's work on the original. Yet Kershner's interest had been piqued, and gradually he came to believe that he could do something with the material - as long as Lucas allowed him the freedom to work in his own style. He didn't simply want to be Lucas's pawn.

With Kershner finally onboard, Lucas now turned to casting. Hamill and Fisher, who had been contracted to three films, would be returning as Luke and Leia, and whilst Harrison Ford hadn't signed such a contract, he also agreed to return as Han Solo after some prevarication. Also onboard were Alec Guinness as the ghostly Obi-Wan Kenobi, Frank Oz, who would be providing the voice and operating the puppet of Yoda, Jeremy Bulloch as Boba Fett, and Billy Dee Williams, who would be playing Solo's rogueish buddy Lando Calrissian (Lucas remembered Williams from the *Star Wars* auditions, when he had tried out for Han Solo). Anthony Daniels, Kenny Baker, Dave Prowse and Peter Mayhew

Carrie Fisher and R2-D2 at the premiere of *The Empire Strikes Back*

would be back too, sweating it out again in their various costumes, all of which had been modified to be more comfortable this time round.

Behind the scenes, Kurtz hired Peter Suschitzky to photograph the movie, whilst Norman Reynolds would be in charge of production design. Paul Hirsch would return to edit, whilst John Williams would again provide the music, Stuart Freeborn the make-up effects, and John Mollo the costumes. With John Dykstra now gone, the effects would be in the hands of Brian Johnson (a veteran of *2001* and TV's *Space: 1999*), plus Richard Edlund, Dennis Muren and Bruce Nicholson, each of whom had risen through the ranks of ILM since assisting Dykstra on *Star Wars*.

With the script complete and all the personnel in place, filming thus began in March 1979. The production was again based at Elstree just outside London (where a new soundstage had been built), and whilst the sets were under construction, the unit flew out to the first location. This was the town of Finse in Norway, the surrounding snow-covered wastes of which would act as a double for the ice planet of Hoth. Unfortunately, the environment proved too realistic, and the production was continually held up by ferocious snowstorms, 40mph winds and temperatures that sometimes fell as low as minus 26 degrees centigrade.

As Lucas had done on *Star Wars*, Kershner storyboarded much of the film. Ralph McQuarrie (who since *Star Wars* had worked on *Battlestar Galactica* and *Lord of the Rings*) again provided the initial artwork, including sketches of the Rebel Command centre and some of the hardware. From these sketches and paintings Kershner worked on the storyboards with Joe Johnston, who was also acting as the conceptual designer for the film's craft (he was responsible for memorable elephant-like AT-AT tanks seen during the battle on Hoth). The storyboards proved invaluable during the Finse shoot, throughout which Kershner stayed in constant touch with ILM back at their new San Rafael headquarters, where Lucas was keeping an eye on the progress of the effects work.

At least valuable time didn't have to be spent on developing the effects equipment from scratch this time. Nevertheless, almost three years had passed since *Star Wars*, and ILM made full use of the advances that had been made in computer technology for *Empire* during that period. Richard Edlund also developed a high speed Vistavision camera and a new optical printer that would help provide superior blue screen composites.

Given the complexity of some of the shots, allied with the bad weather, the shoot in Finse was a slow and laborious process. Nevertheless, it was here that close-ups of Hamill riding his Tauntaun were shot, plus the sequence where he is attacked by a Wampa (this was done to explain Hamill's different look following his car accident). After ten days, Kershner and his cast left for Elstree, leaving behind accomplished second unit director Peter MacDonald to film the remainder of the battle sequences, for which the company hired members of the Norwegian Red Cross Mountain Rescue Team to play the Rebel fighters. A former camera operator, MacDonald had become one of the industry's most reliable second unit directors, and using the storyboards provided by Kershner and Johnston, he made an excellent job of the footage. He later became a fully-fledged director, helming such projects as *Rambo III*, taking over from Russell Mulcahy, *Mo' Money* and *The Neverending Story III*.

Back at Elstree, the newly built stage six held a full-size version of *The Millennium Falcon*. Over the next four months, a total of 64 sets would be built as backgrounds for the film's 250 scenes, one of the most impressive being the swamp planet of Dagobah, home to the eight-hundred-year-old Jedi master Yoda, which had been built on stage three.

Lucas was around for the first two weeks of filming to supervise what was going on, and he returned periodically over the following months. Even in the studio, not everything went to plan. One of the first shots made involved R2-D2 moving through an ice cavern. Unfortunately, the radio-controlled wheels failed to grip the artificial ice on the floor, and the unit had to be pulled along with a nylon cord. Meanwhile, when it came for Luke to raise his X-Wing from the bog on Dagobah using the power of The Force, the wings fell off the craft, owing to the weight of water they'd taken on. Filming in the Carbon Freezing Chamber, built on stage five, also proved hazardous owing the amount of smoke and dry ice needed. Visibilty for the actors and crew was consequently rather poor, which proved dangerous given that parts of the set were over 25 feet off the ground.

There was also plenty of smoke to cloud the actors' vision during the filming of Luke and Darth Vader's sabre fight. A recurring problem on *Star Wars* had been the delicacy of the light sabres, which often broke during filming. This time they had been made from carbon-fibre, so they could be hit without fear of breaking. The fight co-ordinator for the light sabre scene was Bob Anderson, the British Olympic coach and the European sabre champion. Anderson had been hired by the film's stunt co-ordinator Peter Diamond to choreograph the fight, which turned out to be one of the screen's most thrilling. The smoke,

Muppetmeister and Yoda designer Jim Henson with George Lucas during the filming of *Labyrinth*

however, meant that Anderson (who doubled for Dave Prowse) and Hamill (who performed 95 per cent of his own stunts) got their fare share of bumps and bruises while filming. These weren't the only injuries sustained by Hamill. He badly sprained his thumb during the sequence where he falls from the cloud city over Bespin, which meant he had to take several days off while the swelling went down. Adding to all this drama was the news of a plot to kidnap Carrie Fisher. Consequently security on the film and at her home had to be increased, the cost of which came out of the film's budget.

Back on set, the sequences involving Yoda were also proving time consuming, given the minute size of the set of the Jedi master's home. Into this had to fit Mark Hamill, puppeteer Frank Oz (who had to squeeze into a crawl space underneath it), the camera, the camera operator, lights, recording equipment and the director. For all concerned, it was like working in a sauna.

These problems were minor, however, compared to what happened on 6 June

1979. John Barry, the Oscar-winning production designer of *Star Wars*, had been asked by Lucas to work as a second unit director on *Empire*. After his work on *Star Wars*, Barry had designed the sets for *Superman*, after which he attempted to launch his career as a director. Unfortunately, he had been fired from his first film, *Saturn Three*, after just three days by the movie's producer, Stanley Donen, who took over the megaphone himself. It had been Barry's pre-production work for *Saturn Three*, for which he also wrote the story and worked on the design with Stuart Craig, that had prevented him from returning to design *Empire*. At least now he was back in the *Star Wars* fold. Sadly, he collapsed during a meeting with associate producer Robert Watts between shots and died a short time later, the result of a rare form of meningitis.

Barry's death left everyone shocked and upset, and despite the production problems, filming stopped on June 11 for Barry's funeral in Chiswick, at which Gary Kurtz led the tributes to the designer. This one-day stop cost the film $50,000, yet under the circumstances, no one begrudged this, not least Lucas who had been a close friend of Barry's. The next day Kurtz took over Barry's second unit duties (directing the scene in which Luke flees the Wampa cave) until his replacement, Harley Cockliss (future co-writer and director of *Dream Demon)* arrived in London.

It was also in June that Lucas asked editor Paul Hirsch to start work on a rough cut of the footage so far filmed. Lucas was dissatisfied with the results, feeling that the opening sequences at the Rebel base moved too slowly. Re-cutting the footage himself over two days, he pared the scenes down, losing ten minutes of the eighty minutes assembled. Among the casualties were some slow-moving exchanges between Han Solo and Princess Leia. This cut in fact proved to be too fast, and Hirsch subsequently replaced some of the cut footage.

Meanwhile, owing to the delays, the movie's budget was exceeded, and Lucas had to ask the Bank of America for more funds. The bank had also been helping to finance Francis Ford Coppola's *Apocalypse Now*, which had leaped from a provisional $12m to $32m. Consequently, it was a case of being once bitten and twice shy. Despite the certainty that *Empire* would be a hit, the bank refused Lucas's request. Returning to London, Lucas told Kurtz and Kershner to cut back on as many non-essential scenes as possible whilst he tried to raise the money elsewhere. First National of Boston eventually came to the rescue, taking on the Bank of America's commitment. The bank also gave Lucas the additional money he required.

However, it soon became apparent that even *more* money would be needed to finish the film. Now it was time for First National to turn him down - unless, that is, Fox guaranteed the loan. This was the last thing Lucas needed to happen. He just didn't want to be beholden to the studio. Needs must, though, so he approached the studio. Making matters worse was the fact that Lucas's ally Alan Ladd Jr had now left the studio to pursue his own career as a producer (he went on to produce *Body Heat*, *Outland*, *Blade Runner* and *Chariots of Fire* through his own company, The Ladd Company). Consequently, Lucas had to negotiate with the new regime, headed by Sherry Lansing.

Fox was more than happy to guarantee the loan. There was a catch, though. The studio demanded 15 percent of *Empire's* profits. Lucas refused to agree to this term, and instead his lawyer, Tom Pollack, negotiated a new distribution deal with the studio, which also held for the second sequel. Lucas finally had the money he needed to finish the film as he saw fit. At the end of the day, *Empire's* budget, with interest, came in at $39m. Even if it only made 30 percent of the money *Star Wars* had made at the box office, things would work out fine. But there was good news. Bidding from cinemas to show the movie had brought in a record-breaking $26m. The movie wasn't even finished yet, and already it was on the cusp of making a profit.

A deal with Robert Stigwood to release John Williams' *Empire* soundtrack was also negotiated (cutting out Fox completely), while this time toy manufacturers actually approached Lucas and his colleagues, so eager were they to make deals and get on the *Star Wars* bandwagon. Though new deals were made, Lucas remained loyal to Kenner, who continued to produce their lines of character figures and vehicles. Del Rey would provide a novelization again, this time by Donald F. Glut, along with a diary, *Once Upon a Galaxy: A Journal of the Making of The Empire Strikes Back*, by Alan Arnold. Ralph McQuarrie's conceptual work was available, too, in *The Art of The Empire Strikes Back*. *Empire* also spawned the first of what would become a series of computer games, *Star Wars: The Empire Strikes Back*, which was issued by Parker Bros.. An instant hit, it was quickly followed by a second game, *Star Wars: Jedi Arena*.

On August 31, a party was held on the bog planet of Dagobah (suitably re-dressed) to celebrate the completion of principal photography - though obviously much still had to be done with regards to the film's special effects and additional sequences. Among the live action sequences to be filmed were Alec

Guinness's cameo as Obi-Wan Kenobi, plus a close-up of Luke's Tauntan being slit open. Effects-wise, there were the long shots of Luke Skywalker riding the Tauntaun, which were animated frame by frame by Phil Tippett and Jon Berg, who had animated the chess pieces for *Star Wars*. The duo also animated the three AT-AT tanks which are seen during the battle on Hoth. Though they look several storeys high in the movie, the actual height of these AT-AT models was twenty inches. Similarly, the Tauntaun was just sixteen inches high, though an eight foot tall version was also made for the close-ups. Apparently, Lucas approached effects legend Ray Harryhausen (*The Seventh Voyage of Sinbad*, *Jason and the Argonauts*) to animate these sequences. Unfortunately for Lucas, Harryhausen was busy with his own effects epic, *Clash of the Titans*.

Meanwhile, Richard Edlund and the ILM team were beavering away at the effects shots. In the two year period they worked on *Empire*, they produced over 400 shots, which involved the construction of over 50 miniatures. All told, some 120 hours of effects shots and live action was filmed for *The Empire Strikes Back*, all of which had to be edited down to an action-packed 124 minutes. To all of this, Ben Burtt then had to add his sound effects, whilst James Earl Jones again returned to dub the voice of Darth Vader. During the filming of the scene in which Vader reveals that he is Skywalker's father, Dave Prowse had actually been told to say that it was in fact Obi-Wan Kenobi who was Skywalker's father. Only at the premier of the movie did a somewhat disgruntled Prowse discover the switch.

Then, between 27 December 1979 and 18 January 1980, John Williams recorded his score for the movie using 129 members of The London Symphony Orchestra. Since *Star Wars*, Williams had worked with the orchestra on *Superman*, *Dracula* and the album for *The Fury*. Given their superb work on all these projects, Williams was happy to use them again on *Empire*. This time the composer produced the sessions himself (which, as always, he also conducted), again working with orchestrator Herbert W. Spencer, recording supervisor Lionel Newman and recording engineer Eric Tomlinson.

As before, Williams adopted the *leitmotif* technique for his score, and though the main themes from *Star Wars* returned (the *Main Title March*, Luke and Leia's themes), much of his music was new. This included a lilting theme for Yoda and a Wagnerian playground taunt for Darth Vader (who'd been denied his own theme in *Star Wars*). One of Williams' most brilliant scores, there were many virtuoso passages of writing on display, notably the superbly orchestrated *Asteroid Field*, which remains one of the most exhilarating pieces of music ever written for the movies. Williams's score, recorded at both Anvil Studios and Abbey Road, went on sale on 16 May 1980, five days before the movie opened in theatres in America. A double-disc gatefold album containing 75 minutes of the film's music, it went on to sell over one million copies by August of the same year.

Whilst Williams was working on his score, the advertising department was going into overdrive as the movie's 21 May release came ever closer. Lucas had complete control over the advertising this time, and wanted the film's poster to appeal to women as well as men. With this in mind, designer Roger Kastel produced a *Gone with the Wind*-style piece of artwork featuring Princess Leia in the arms of Han Solo. Luke was also featured on his Tauntaun, along with C-3PO, R2-D2, Chewbacca and Darth Vader, whilst a second edition of the poster included Lando Calrissian and Boba Fett. The tag line was simple and to the point. 'The *Star Wars* saga continues.'

Trailers had also been playing in cinemas since Christmas 1979, whilst on 29 March 1980, Mark Hamill guested on the ever-popular *Muppet Show* as both himself and Luke Skywalker, in which he encountered Fozzie Bear and Miss Piggy (both, of course, voiced and operated by Yoda himself, Frank Oz). Anthony Daniels also popped up as C-3PO, whilst extras were hired to don the costumes of Darth Vader (no doubt much to Dave Prowse's chagrin), Chewbacca and R2-D2. By now, audience anticipation for the new movie was at fever pitch...

14

The Empire Strikes Back – And Then Some!

The hem of Darth Vader's cloak is caked with dust as he wafts about the command bridge of The Executor.

The insignia of several characters aboard The Executor *inexplicably change lapels within the space of one sequence.*

In the original Empire Strikes Back *(not the* Special Edition*) one can see through the aircraft during the battle of Hoth, owing to poor matting.*

The Empire Strikes Back was released on the Wednesday before Memorial Day, a date Lucas now saw as lucky following the release of *Star Wars* on that same date three years earlier. Instead of 8am in the morning, though, queues for the new movie began forming at some cinemas three days before the opening.

This time, instead of a paltry 32 cinemas, *Empire* opened wide in 127 theatres (still a small number by late nineties standards), at which it broke house records at 125 of them. By the end of the first week the movie had grossed $9m domestically. By the end of the month this had risen to $31m, and prior to the *Special Edition* re-release, the total US box office for *Empire* came in at a highly respectable $170m. Worldwide the take was in excess of $300m.

As with *Star Wars*, *Empire* left contemporary releases such as *Fame*, *Can't Stop the Music* and *The Blues Brothers* (in which Carrie Fisher had a small role) standing. Of the huge sums the movie made, Fox took a $40m wedge for releasing it, whilst Lucasfilm made $51m in profit. Add to this the phenomenal merchandising sales, and Lucas's wage packet for the movie - given that he was the chairman and sole shareholder of Lucasfilm - was in excess of $100m. His dream of building his studio complex, The Skywalker Ranch out in Marin County, was now a reality.

Again, Lucas was the man of the moment, and found characters from his movie on the covers of both *Time Magazine* (Darth Vader) and *People Magazine* (Yoda). An honour indeed. If anything, the reviews were even more favourable than they had been for *Star Wars*. 'From the first burst of John Williams' powerful score and the receding opening title crawl, we are back in pleasant surroundings and anxious for a good time,' said *Variety*. Added Pauline Kael, who'd been somewhat tepid towards *Star Wars*, 'You can feel the love of movie magic that went into its cascading imagery.' The British press was also enthusiastic, none more so than *The Sunday Telegraph*, which trumpeted, 'As the successor to *Star Wars* it is every bit as visually astounding, fast-moving, noisy, swashbuckling and unbelievable as its parent.'

As he'd been with *Star Wars*, John Simon was one of the few critics not to be swayed by the movie, moaning 'Infantile is the operative word. This witless banality is made even less bearable by the non-acting of the principals. Harrison Ford offers loutishness for charm... Mark Hamill is still the talentless Tom Sawyer of outer space - wide-eyed, narrow-minded, strait-laced. Worst of all is Carrie Fisher, whose Leia is a cosmic Shirley Temple but without the slightest acting ability or vestige of prettiness. Though still very young, she looks, without recourse to special effects, at least fifty.' Ouch! Simon concluded his review by commenting, 'The program lists five-and-a-half pages of credits; it would take at least twice that space to list the debits.'

As he had done with *Star Wars*, Lucas rewarded his cast and crew with bonuses, among them the staff at ILM and Lucasfilm. He also gave points in the movie to Kenny Baker and Peter Mayhew. More importantly, Lucas was also able to pay back his huge bank loans. Not everyone came out of the process smiling, though. A distance had grown between Lucas and his producer Gary Kurtz, whom Lucas held responsible for the time and budgetary overruns on *Empire*. As a consequence, Kurtz decided that now, after three highly successful movies with Lucas, it was time to go his own way. This he did, joining forces with Jim Henson and his company to produce a fantasy titled *Dark Crystal*, which would go on to be co-directed by Muppetmeister Henson and Frank Oz.

Lucas did go some way to mending bridges with Irvin Kershner, however. During the shoot of *Empire* he'd been perplexed by the slowness of Kershner's working methods (Kershner actually talked to the actors, unlike Lucas). Lucas also had disliked the way Kershner had paced the movie, which the director had seen as having three distinct movements; the first fast, the second slower, the third picking up the pace again. It was only once the film was on release that Lucas finally saw the wisdom of this. The result was an exhilarating inter-planetary adventure that was carried by three-dimensional characters as opposed to the special effects, good as they were.

Both critics and fans seemed to agree that *The Empire Strikes Back* was every bit as good - if not better - than *Star Wars*. It certainly had more depth and texture to it. Like the second act of a grand opera, it also had a tragic ending. We don't know what is to become of Han Solo, last seen being carbon frozen. One could say it was the most expensive serial cliffhanger ever made.

Not all was plain sailing for the movie, though. The Director's Guild of America, of which both Lucas and Kershner were members, informed Lucas that he was in line for a $250,000 fine for failing to credit Kershner at the top of the film. As had been the case with *Star Wars*, there were no credits at the beginning of the film; simply the Fox and Lucasfilm logos. Kershner himself had no problem with this, understanding that this was part of the house style (Lucas, after all, hadn't been credited until the end of either picture). The DGA would not relent, however, and when Lucas threatened to take them to court, they warned him that if he lost his case, then they would also fine Kershner for working for Lucasfilm, as the company didn't have a DGA contract. Outraged at the foolishness of the entire situation, Lucas settled the matter out of court, eventually paying a fine of $25,000. He also had to cough up an additional

$15,000 to the Writers' Guild, of which he was also a member, for inadequately crediting Lawrence Kasdan. The money was peanuts to Lucas. It was the principle of the thing. If anything, it made him even more determined to cut his ties with Hollywood.

In late 1980, work had started the Skywalker Ranch. The move from Tinseltown was now just a matter of time, and with that in mind Lucas resigned his membership from the DGA, the Writers' Guild and the Academy of Motion Picture Arts and Sciences in April the following year. That same month *Star Wars* was re-released for a third time (*Empire* itself would also be re-released on 31 July).

By this time Academy Awards had been and gone. Though *The Empire Strikes Back* didn't quite sweep the board as had *Star Wars*, it was nevertheless nominated in four categories: original score (John Williams), art direction and set decoration (Norman Reynolds, Leslie Dilley, Harry Lange, Alan Tomkins, Michael Ford), sound (Bill Varney, Steve Maslow, Gregg Landaker, Peter Sutton), and special effects (Brian Johnson, Richard Edlund, Dennis Muren, Bruce Nicholson). The film eventually went on to win two of these: best sound and best effects, losing best score to *Fame* (Michael Gore), and best art direction to *Tess* (Pierre Guffroy, Jack Stevens). Across the pond in Britain, *Empire* also won a BAFTA for best score (John Williams).

Meanwhile, *Star Wars* was adapted for the radio by Brain Daley (who had worked on a trilogy of Han Solo books). This 13-part series, which was scripted between December 1979 and March 1980, was co-produced by National Public Radio and Southern California's KUSC-FM, and was regarded as part of the official *Star Wars* canon by Lucas, who sold the radio rights for just one dollar. It included 30 new scenes, all of which were cleared by Lucas himself, the one exception being a brief moment in the Rebel hangar in which Leia notices Han's scarred back. Jabba was also changed to a character called Heater. Mark Hamill returned to play Luke Skywalker, along with Anthony Daniels as C-3PO. However, Perry King (known for *Slaughterhouse Five* and *Lipstick*) took on the mantle of Han Solo, whilst Ann Sachs played Princess Leia and Brock Peters (best known for his roles in *To Kill a Mockingbird* and *The L-Shaped Room*) took over from James Earl Jones as Darth Vader.

The programmes produced the biggest response in the network's history, generating 50,000 letters and phone calls in just one week. Each episode pulled

Carrie Fisher and Billy Dee Williams during the launch of the *Special Editions* in an astonishing 750,000 listeners, a 40 percent increase in the network's audience. The critics were enthusiastic too, *The LA Times* commenting that the programmes were, 'Fun, sping-tingling, mind-bending pieces of escapist entertainment that don't miss the visuals a bit.' Given this success, Lucas announced that *The Empire Strikes Back* would receive the same treatment.

Disco king Meco Monardo also got in on the *Star Wars* action again. However, if he hoped that his *Star Wars* Christmas album *Christmas in the Stars* would out-sell his disco version of the *Star Wars* theme he was sadly mistaken. Apparently, the idea was to produce an LP of festive favourites to rival the likes of *Rudolph the Red-Nosed Reindeer*. Things didn't quite work out that way, though, and one of the numbers, *What Can You Get a Wookiee for Christmas (When He Already Has a Comb)?* would later return to haunt its singer, a young Jon Bonjovi. Astonishingly, Lucas okayed the album.

Despite all this activity, Lucas's film commitments were gradually taking him away from the *Star Wars* universe, though proposals for the third film in the central trilogy were already being mooted. There was even a title circulating: *Revenge of the Jedi*. Yet there were other projects to consider, among them an animated piece called *Twice Upon a Time*. There was also Lucas's idea for a serial-like adventure based on the exploits of an archaeologist, which was beginning to take shape. But would audiences be interested in a Lucas movie that didn't feature Han, Luke and Leia?

15

Whip Crack Away!

*During the drinking competition in Marion's bar, a cockney extra can
clearly be heard exclaiming, "Give 'im space! Give 'im space!"
However, the scene is supposedly set in the outer reaches of Nepal.*

*R2-D2 and C-3PO can been seen as heiroglyphics
in the Well of Souls sequence.*

Producer Frank Marshall appears as the Nazi pilot of the Flying Wing.

*At the climax of the opening sequence, Indy escapes in a plane with the
registration OB-CPO, a reference to both Obi-Wan Kenobi and C-3PO.*

*The opening Paramount logo segues into a Peruvian mountain
which looks exactly the same.*

Given his admiration of Akira Kurosawa, whose films he had partially drawn
upon when scripting *Star Wars*, it was perhaps inevitable that Lucas would use
his newly acquired power and good fortune to help the Japanese director secure

the financing he'd been having trouble raising to mount his latest epic, *Kagemusha* (aka *The Shadow Warrior*).

Teaming up with Francis Ford Coppola, Lucas earned himself an executive producer credit on the international release of the movie, which centred round a clan chief's double taking over his role after his death. A spectacular production with some stunning battle sequences, the finished film was regarded as an instant classic by many critics, earning a best foreign film nomination from the Academy of Motion Picture Arts and Sciences, along with a best director BAFTA statuette for Kurosawa himself. Without Lucas and Coppola's help, the world might never have seen this brilliant film. But then again, Lucas had always been determined to put back into the industry as much as he had got out of it.

Meanwhile, closer to home, there was the matter of *Raiders of the Lost Ark*, which Lucas had been developing alongside *The Empire Strikes Back*. With *Empire* now out of the way he could concentrate fully on the project. Of course, it had been on the boil for some time, even before that vacation in Hawaii in 1977 following the opening of *Star Wars,* when Lucas had discussed his idea with Steven Spielberg. In fact he'd already done some work on the story by this point, having developed ideas with his friend, writer-director Philip Kaufman, who was then known primarily for his work on *The Great Northfield Minesota Raid* (though he'd go on to make such admired films as *The Right Stuff*, *The Unbearable Lightness of Being* and *Rising Sun*). However, this work had been put aside when Kaufman went off to co-script *The Outlaw Josey Wales* for director-star Clint Eastwood.

Cut to the late seventies. Spielberg was keen to get involved in Lucas's idea, even more so following the box office disaster of his lavish World War Two comedy *1941*, which had run vastly over schedule and budget. Keen to prove that he could bring a movie in on time and on budget, Spielberg was more than happy to take up Lucas's offer to direct the movie, especially, as like Lucas, he was a big fan of the old cliffhanging serials. Originally, Spielberg had set his heart on directing a Bond movie. However, Lucas assured him that their movie would pretty much out-strip Bond in every department.

It had been Philip Kaufman who had suggested that the story revolve round the search for the lost Ark of the Covenant and its contents, the tablets on which the Ten Commandments had been inscribed. This gave the story an added resonance, especially given that the Nazis are also pursuing the Ark for its legendary powers. Working to this end, Lucas and Spielberg decided that the movie should be one long extended chase, with the Nazis and the hero constantly interchanging roles as pursuer and pursued.

As with *Star Wars*, many ideas came and went. The hero, originally named Indiana Smith, was at first to have been a Manhattan playboy who sidelines in archeology to finance his lavish lifestyle. It was only after some consideration that Indiana Jones, as he was finally known, became a college professor constantly on the hunt for ancient artefacts, leading him into adventure after adventure. A blend of James Bond and Cary Grant, he was the ultimate movie hero: dashing, brave and with a nonchalant sense of humour.

As he had been on *The Empire Strikes Back*, Lucas was the executive producer on *Raiders of the Lost Ark*, along with Howard Kazanjian, who had produced *More American Graffiti* for him. To actually produce the movie Lucas turned to Frank Marshall, whose first major credit *Raiders* would be. Born in 1947, Marshall began his career as an assistant director for Peter Bogdanovich, working on *Targets* and *The Last Picture Show*, in both of which he also appeared. He then graduated to associate producer with *Paper Moon*, *Daisy Miller*, *Nickelodeon* (all for Bogdanovich) and *The Warriors*. Following his work on *Raiders* (in which he can be spotted as the pilot whom Marion knocks out on the Flying Wing), he went on to form Amblin Entertainment with his wife, Kathleen Kennedy (who worked on *Raiders* as Steven Spielberg's 'associate') and Spielberg himself. Between them the triumvirate would make some of the most popular movies of the eighties, among them the *Back to the Future* trilogy, *Gremlins* and *Who Framed Roger Rabbit?* Marshall eventually gravitated towards direction, having helmed the second unit sequences on *Indiana Jones and the Temple of Doom*, *Back to the Future*, *Indiana Jones and the Last Crusade*, *The Color Purple* and *Always*, making his debut with *Arachnophobia*, which he followed with *Alive* and *Congo*. Clearly ambitious, he was the ideal candidate to produce *Raiders*.

Once Lawrence Kasdan had completed the script, Lucas took it to Michael Eisner at Paramount, convincing the studio head that the elaborate production could be made for under $20m - quite a claim given that the movie would be shooting in four countries, with the interiors being filmed at Elstree. Penalty clauses were thus put into the contract if the movie went over schedule and budget. Consequently, everyone was ordered to keep costs down. With this in mind, Spielberg storyboarded pretty much all of the film, providing crude thumbnail sketches which were then turned into full-blown drawings by a team of artists, among them Roy Carnon, Ron Cobb, Dave Negron, Ed Verreaux and Ron Croci. Jim Steranko also provided a production painting of Indy in action to help convey the flavour of the film to Paramount's executives, whilst Michael Lloyd did a number of oil paintings highlighting key scenes.

Turning to casting his hero, Lucas first opted for television star Tom Selleck, then enjoying his biggest success with the action series *Magnum PI*. However, when CBS learned that Lucas was interested in poaching Selleck for a movie, they refused to release him from his contract. Though Selleck would eventually go on to make a number of movies, among them the *Raiders*-like *High Road to China* and *Three Men and a Baby*, he never became the first rank movie star that *Raiders* might have made him. Consequently, Lucas turned to Harrison Ford to portray Indy.

There would be no light sabre for Ford to get Indy out of sticky situations with here, though. The movie was set in 1936, so Indy would have to rely on his bullwhip and his instincts. Yet despite the period setting, the film would not be without its lavish effects sequences, most notably the climax in which the Ark erupts in fury, killing the Nazis who have dared to try and use its powers for their own evil ends. Naturally, ILM handled all the movie's effects. Among the effects technicians working on the movie would be several *Empire Strikes Back* veterans, among them Richard Edlund, Bruce Nicholson and Joe Johnston (who had storyboarded *Empire*), whilst Kit West was added to the team to handle all the on-site physical effects, which included gun shots, explosions and fireballs.

Meanwhile, Peter Diamond (also an *Empire* veteran) and Glenn Randall handled the movie's endless stream of stunts. Among the more spectacular of these featured Indy moving from the front of a moving truck to the back, via the undercarriage. Much of this spectacular sequence was handled by second unit director Michael Moore and photographed by British cameraman Paul Beeson, with stunt double Vic Armstrong replacing Ford. This was the first time Steven Spielberg had used a second unit director. He preferred to be behind the camera for every shot in his films. Yet if he was to bring the movie in on time, and get all the required sequences in the can, this was the only way to do it, though obviously Moore was working to Spielberg's strict instructions. However, whilst life and limb were being risked to achieve all the incredible stunts, the hardest thing the crew had to contend with was keeping Indy's hat on during each take. This was achieved by lining the hat with sticky tape, though even this didn't always work, and it would fly off at the least appropriate moment, ruining a take.

On the main unit, Spielberg was supported by distinguished British cinematographer Douglas Slocombe, with whom he had worked before on the India sequences for *Close Encounters of the Third Kind*. Born in 1913, Slocombe was something of an industry legend, having worked on such Ealing classics as *The Lavender Hill Mob* and *The Man in the White Suit*. In the sixties he photographed such productions as *The Blue Max*, *The Lion in Winter* and *The Italian Job*, all of which made him ideal for photographing Indy's exploits.

Many of the film's supporting cast were also British. Among them were Paul Freeman as villain in chief Belloq, Denholm Elliott as Indy's friend Marcus Brody, Ronald Lacey as henchman Toht, Alfred Molina as the duplicitous Satipo and John Rhys-Davies as the helpful Sallah. Actor and stuntman Pat Roach even got to play two parts: a Sherpa who becomes involved in the fracas in the Nepalese bar, and the German mechanic with whom Indy has a particularly brutal fist fight on the Flying Wing. One of the few Americans in the cast was Karen Allen, who as Indy's lost love Marion Ravenwood was a feisty damsel in distress in the Princess Leia mould.

Shooting on the movie began on 23 June 1980 in La Rochelle where, for a week, Spielberg and his crew shot the scenes onboard the tramp steamer Bantu Wind and the German submarine. For the full scale shots of the sub, one inherited from *Das Boot* was used, whilst for longer shots the miniature sub from *1941* was used. The projected schedule for the entire movie was 22 weeks, though Spielberg's break-neck speed whittled this down to a brisk fifteen weeks, much to Lucas's pleasure. As well as location work in France and North Africa, the film also visited Tunisia, where the canyon in which R2-D2 is captured by the Jawas in *Star Wars* was again made use of. This time the canyon was used for a scene towards the end of the movie in which Indy holds the Germans up with a rocket launcher. Some shots for this scene were actually directed by George Lucas, who was often on set. Lucas also directed an insert shot of Barranca's monkey doing a Nazi salute.

The Tunisian canyon (dubbed *Star Wars* canyon by Lucas) wasn't the only *Star Wars* reference in *Raiders of the Lost Ark*. C-3PO and R2-D2 were also featured as hieroglyphics on the walls in the Well of Souls (though they're pretty hard to spot). One of the least comfortable sequences for the cast and crew to film, the Well of Souls featured a thirty-seven foot high statue of an Egyptian jackal god and made use of some 6500 live reptiles, among them pythons, boa constrictors and cobras. Given these circumstances, a snake expert with five assistants was always on set, along with a medical team with the required antidotes. The film also made use of 50 live tarantulas which were used in the Bond-style opening sequence in which Indy and Satipo attempt to steal a gold idol from an ancient booby-trapped Peruvian tomb. To assure his cast everything was safe, Spielberg himself personally put the creatures on the back of Alfred Molina for one shot that required the actor to be covered with the hairy arachnids.

Keen to make his portrayal of the adventure-loving Indy as believable as possible, Harrison Ford did much work with the stunt co-ordinators, immediately hitting it off with his double Vic Armstrong (a veteran of *Superman* and several Bond films). He also learned to use his bullwhip proficiently. However, one elaborate scene in which Indy was to have used his whip in a fight against a broadsword-wielding thug ended up being dropped as Ford had dysentry and didn't have the strength to film the scene. Instead the actor suggested that Indy simply shoot the villain, thus saving four shooting days. Spielberg agreed, and the scene as filmed produces the biggest laugh in the film.(Other accounts of the movie maintain that the shooting incident was in the screenplay all along, suggesting that Ford's supposed script change 'on the floor' was in fact a piece of shrewd publicity for the film's leading man.)

Joining Ford on location was his second wife Melissa Matheson, who struck up a friendship with producer Frank Marshall's wife Kathleen Kennedy. This friendship eventually led to Matheson scripting *E.T.* (then known as *A Boy's Life*) for Spielberg and Kennedy. Ford even had a small role in this film as a teacher, though it ended up on the cutting room floor.

Meanwhile, as filming gradually came to a conclusion, Lucas began to supervise the editing of the movie, which was in the expert hands of Spielberg's regular editor Michael Kahn. Again, Ben Burtt returned to provide the film's many sound effects, among them the exaggerated comic book-style punches, many of which Indy receives during the film. Also returning was composer John Williams, who again outdid himself by providing the movie with another instantly identifiable theme, *The Raiders March*. Williams recorded the score in London in February 1981, dividing sessions between the Anvil Recording Studios and Abbey Road. Lucas, Spielberg, Frank Marshall and Kathleen Kennedy were on hand for these recordings, which were supervised by Lionel Newman, orchestrated by Herbert W. Spencer and recorded and mixed by Eric Tomlinson.

Hype for the movie was also building up. To design the poster, Lucas hired the talented Amsel, whose campaigns for *Murder on the Orient Express* and *Death on the Nile* had proved both eye-catching and in keeping with those films' thirties settings. Amsel again came up trumps with his design for *Raiders*, which centred round a full portrait of Indy, complete with his trademark Fedora and bullwhip.

When it was finally released on 12 June 1981, *Raiders* was an instant hit, generating a US gross of $231m. Its success also confirmed Harrison Ford as a front rank star. The reviews were also highly positive. '*Raiders of the Lost Ark* is the stuff that raucous Saturday matinees at the local Bijou once were made of,' cooed *Variety*, adding, 'Director Steven Spielberg has deftly veiled proceedings in a sense of mystical wonder that makes it all the more easy for viewers to suspend belief and settle back for the fun.' Added the *Hollywood Reporter*, 'If George Lucas were to say that he could make a terrific entertainment out of Chairman Mao's *Little Red Book*, at this point I'd be inclined to believe him.'

The biggest amount of praise came from Roger Ebert, whose review was practically a love letter to Lucas and Spielberg. He described *Raiders* as being, 'An out of body experience, a movie of glorious imagination and breakneck speed that grabs you through a series of incredible adventures, and deposits you back in reality two hours later breathless, dizzy, wrung out, and with a silly grin on your face. Britain's *Sight and Sound* was less enamoured, though, commenting that the film was, 'Both *de trop* and not enough.' Audiences didn't pay these derisory comments any heed, and flocked to the movie in their millions, welcoming the return of the good humoured action adventure. James Bond, it seemed, now had some serious competition.

In addition to its success with audiences around the world, *Raiders* also did well on the awards circuit. It earned eight Oscar nominations in all, including best picture, best director (Spielberg), best editing (Michael Kahn), best music (John Williams), best art direction and set decoration (Norman Reynolds, Leslie Dilley, Michael Ford), best cinematography (Douglas Slocombe), best sound (Bill Varney, Steve Maslow, Gregg Landaker, Roy Charman) and best visual effects (Richard Edlund, Kit West, Joe Johnston and Bruce Nicholson). It went on to win the award in four of these categories: for editing, art direction, sound and visual effects. It also won a special achievement award for Ben Burtt and Richard L. Anderson's sound effects editing. The movie also won a BAFTA for Norman Reynolds art direction.

As the eighties were shaping up, Lucas's trophy cabinet was beginning to look decidedly full. His bank balance was looking very healthy too. And with the third *Star Wars* film still to come, things could only get better.

16
Time for Revenge

A TIE Fighter flies through the Millennium Falcon during the battle sequence in Return of the Jedi *owing to a mistake in the matting process.*

Three of Jabba's henchmen are named Klaatu, Barada and Nikto after the much-used phrase from The Day the Earth Stood Still.

Richard Marquand and Frank Watts appear briefly as pilots of an AT-ST.

During the build up to the filming of the third *Star Wars* movie, Lucas involved himself in a couple of other projects. The first of these was the sultry film noir thriller *Body Heat*, though he didn't take any credit for his involvement. The film marked the directorial debut of Lawrence Kasdan, following his screenwriting duties on *Continental Divide*, *The Empire Strikes Back* and *Raiders of the Lost Ark*. In effect, Lucas sponsored Kasdan's debut, standing in the shadows should the film run into problems, just as Francis Ford Coppola had helped Lucas secure *American Graffiti*. The film's backers, headed by Alan Ladd Jr, who released the film through Warner Bros. and his newly formed Ladd Company, need not have worried about Kasdan's abilities though,

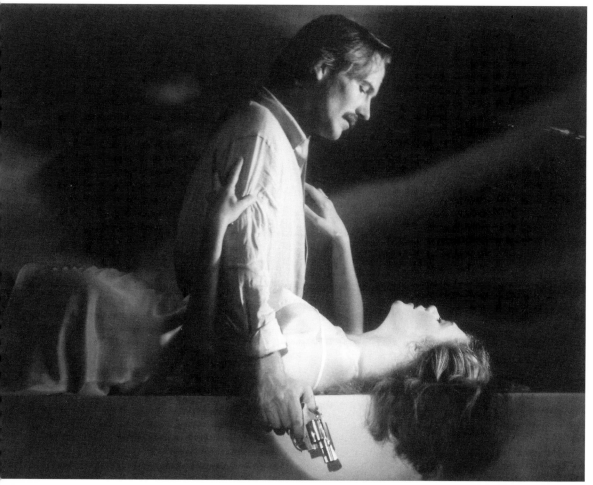

Body Heat: the heat increases. Kathleen Turner entangles William Hurt in a web of passion and deceit. Lucas anonymously executive produced the film.

for he delivered a classy thriller on the lines of *Double Indemnity*, making stars of William Hurt and Kathleen Turner in the process.

Smoothly photographed in Florida by Richard H. Kline, *Body Heat* also benefited from an excellent John Barry score (though it was John Williams who provided the new Ladd Company musical logo). The film also featured early performances by Ted Danson and Mickey Rourke. A commercial success, it was Kasdan's stepping stone to the big time, and it earned him some excellent reviews. '*Body Heat* is an engrossing, mightily stylish meller in which sex and crime walk hand in hand down the path to tragedy, just like in the old days,' commented *Variety*.

Less successful was Lucas's involvement, as executive producer, with the animated feature *Twice Upon a Time*, which never received a full theatrical release. Co-directed by Charles Swenson and Lucas's buddy John Korty (who already had made such live action films as *Funnyman*, *The Autobiography of Miss Jane Pittman* and *Oliver's Story*), the film made use of a process known as 'lumage', which involved the animation of cut out shapes and characters which are lit from below. Financed again by Alan Ladd Jr to the tune of $3m, the film centred round an evil character called Synonamess Botch and his plot to turn people's dreams to nightmares - only to be foiled in his plan by a group of eccentric heroes, who include one Rod Rescueman.

Unfortunately, the film wasn't primarily aimed at children, and adult audiences in 1982 had yet to accept animation as anything other than kiddy fare. Perhaps had *Twice Upon a Time* been made during the resurgence of Disney animation in the late eighties and early nineties, its quirky style might have met with greater success, as did Tim Burton's later effort *The Nightmare Before Christmas*. As it was, the film quickly sank without trace.

But Lucas had his fingers in too many pies to worry too much about the film's failure. By now, ILM was doing effects work on a number of non-Lucas projects, among them *Dragonslayer*, *The Dark Crystal*, *Star Trek II: The Wrath of Khan*, *Poltergeist* and *E.T.*, the latter of which won an Academy Award for best special effects. Lucas's Skywalker Sound company, the home of the newly developed THX Sound, was also gaining respect for its work on the likes of *E.T.* and *Koyaanisqatsi*.

All the while Lucas was working on the development of the story for the new *Star Wars* film, to be called *The Revenge of the Jedi*. Perhaps because he'd secured his directorial debut on *Body Heat*, Lucas was able to persuade Lawrence Kasdan to return to the fold one last time to script *Jedi* with him, which Kasdan was happy to do. Then there was the question of who would direct the film. Irvin Kershner was in the midst of directing the rogue Bond film *Never Say Never Again*, so was out of the picture, though given their differences on *Empire* it's not likely that Lucas gave Kershner serious consideration.

In fact at the top of Lucas's list to direct *Jedi* was Steven Spielberg, with whom he'd enjoyed working enormously on *Raiders*. However, the fact that Lucas had resigned from the Director's Guild of America meant that, ostensibly, he had to hire a non-DGA member to helm the movie, which put Spielberg out of the running. For a time Lucas considered hiring David Lynch, hot after his success with *The Elephant Man*, but finally elected to follow another path - leaving Lynch free to helm another space epic, the commercially disastrous *Dune*.

After interviewing another twelve potential candidates for the job, Lucas then rather surprisingly turned to a Welshman, Richard Marquand, to direct. Best known for his 1971 television drama-documentary series *The Search for the Nile*, Marquand, who was born in 1938, had turned to features in 1978 with variable success, first with the lacklustre shocker *The Legacy*, which he followed with *The Birth of the Beatles* (for American television) and the rather better World War Two spy thriller *Eye of the Needle*. The foregone success of *Jedi* would place him among the front rank of Hollywood directors.

With Marquand, who proved pliable to Lucas's vision for the movie, now onboard, Lucas and Kasdan began working with the director in earnest on the shape of the story, which Kasdan and Lucas then scripted between them. As always, this script was then storyboarded in detail. In the meantime, Howard Kazanjian, who was to produce the film following his firm grip of the *Raiders'* budget, began preparing a number of key locations ready for the start of filming, among them an area of desert near Yuma in Arizona, and a stretch of woodland in Crescent City, California.

Also busy was ILM effects animator Phil Tippett, who since working on *Star Wars* and *Empire*, had helped to design the dragons for *Dragonslayer*. On *Jedi* he graduated to being responsible for the creation of all the new creatures with Stuart Freeborn, among them the slug-like Jabba the Hutt (the human version of which had been cut from *Star Wars*) and the teddybear-like Ewoks. Working with artists Ralph McQuarrie, Joe Johnston and Nilo Rodis-Jamero (who would also co-design the film's costumes with Aggie Guerard Rodgers), Tippett spent almost twelve months working on creature concepts, all of which then had to be realised by a crew of creature technicians.

Other technicians and designers were also being assembled for *Jedi*, among them production designer Norman Reynolds, back again after his Oscar-winning success on *Raiders*, and British cinematographer Alan Hume, who had so far photographed all of director Richard Marquand's movies. Born in 1924, Hume was both prolific and fast-working, beginning his career as a camera operator on the *Carry On* comedies and TV's *The Avengers* before becoming a lighting cameraman. As such he would go on to photograph a wide variety of movies, among them *Carry On Cruising*, *At the Earth's Core* and *Wombling Free*, before graduating to bigger budgeted pictures such as *Bear Island* and the Bond film *For Your Eyes Only*. Photographing *Jedi* would prove to be a career high for Hume, who as a consequence went on to make two more Bonds (*Octopussy* and *A View to a Kill*) and such high profile films as *Supergirl*,

Runaway Train, *A Fish Called Wanda* and *Shirley Valentine*.

Effects-wise, the ILM team was this time headed by Richard Edlund, Dennis Muren, Ken Ralston and Phil Tippett, who would create the 900 effects shots needed for the film, using up $10m of the film's estimated $30m budget. Meanwhile, in the editing rooms, Lucas's wife Marcia, along with Sean Barton and Duwayne Dunham, toiled away on getting all these shots into shape.

As they had done in *The Empire Strikes Back*, all the principals returned to repeat their roles. Since *Empire*, Mark Hamill had acted in a number of plays, among them *The Elephant Man* and *Amadeus*, in which he'd played Mozart. He'd also made a disappointing film, *The Night the Lights Went Out in Georgia*, which had centred round a girl's attempts to turn her hick brother (played by Dennis Quaid) into a country and western singer. Carrie Fisher had similarly worked on stage in *Agnes of God*, though like Hamill, her film career hadn't taken off, her only appearance on screen being in the disappointing Chevy Chase comedy *Under the Rainbow*, which told the behind the scenes story of the filming of *The Wizard of Oz* from the point of view of the midgets playing the Munchkins. Only Harrison Ford had scored a success with *Raiders*, which he'd then followed with the commercially unsuccessful cult movie *Blade Runner*.

Also back were Billy Dee Williams as Lando Calrissian, Frank Oz as Yoda, Alec Guinness (very briefly) as the ghostly Obi-Wan Kenobi, Anthony Daniels as C-3PO, Kenny Baker as R2-D2, Dave Prowse as Darth Vader (again voiced by James Earl Jones) and Peter Mayhew as Chewbacca.

This time the story revolves round Luke coming to terms with the fact that his father is Darth Vader, and his temptation to join him on the dark side. The film opens with Leia a captive of Jabba the Hutt. Leia and Solo, who is thawed from his carbon tomb, are rescued by Luke. Following a fight on Jabba's Sail Barge, the Rebels again take up the cudgels with Vader, the Empire and its evil Emperor, who are in the process of building a new Death Star. However, help is at hand in the form of the Ewoks, and the Rebels use their woodland planet, Endor, as a base to destroy the new Death Star. As in *The Empire Strikes Back*, there is also another soap opera-style revelation: Leia, it transpires, is Luke's sister!

Some felt the introduction of the Emperor (played by Ian McDiarmid) somewhat diluted Vader's role as villain-in-chief, as did the fact that we finally see what Vader looks like under his black helmet. Especially as it isn't Dave Prowse under there, but a third actor, Sebastian Shaw, who plays Vader's alter

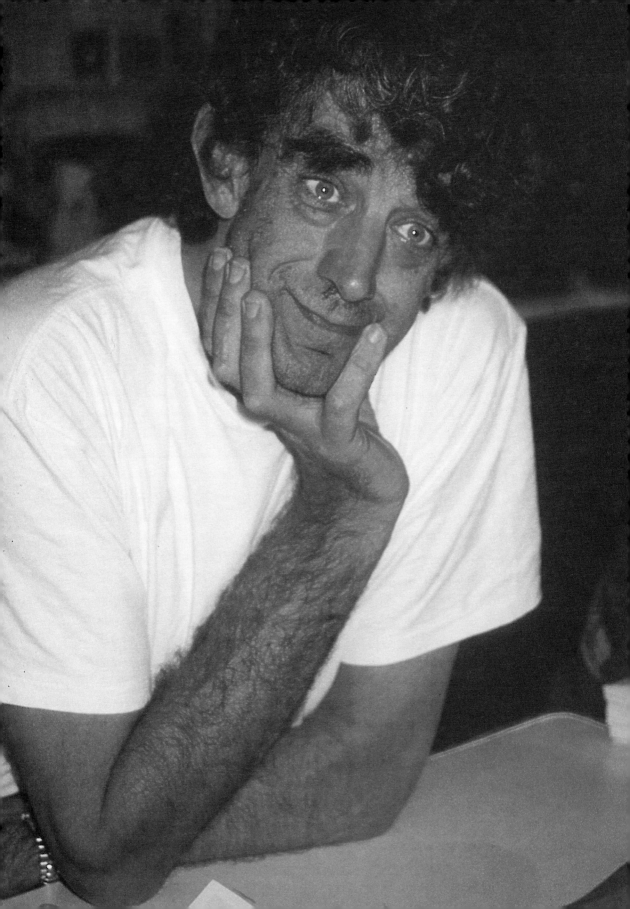

ego Anakin Skywalker. Hamill himself, meanwhile, expressed concerns that Luke's walk with the Dark Side was too easily resolved, quickly being sacrificed for the inevitable up-beat ending the third installment demanded.

All these plot twists and revelations were kept as secret as possible during filming, so much so that during the shoot at Elstree, which began on 11 January 1982, scripts and call sheets carried the title *Blue Harvest*, supposedly a horror movie. Even crew members were issue with tee-shirts bearing the legend 'Blue Harvest - Horror Beyond Imagination!' though inevitably the ruse didn't last for long, despite another purposefully manufactured rumour that the movie was being made in Germany. Despite all these precautions, only Lucas, Marquand and Kazanjian were in posession of the film's complete script. Even Ford, Fisher and Hamill only got to learn of some of the plot twists on the actual day of shooting them, often to their consternation and irritation.

As it had been for *Star Wars*, *The Empire Strikes Back* and *Raiders of the Lost Ark*, Elstree was used to film the movie's interiors, and all nine stages were used to house such sets as Jabba the Hutt's palace, the Rebel hangar, the Death Star docking bay, a full-size Imperial shuttle, the Emperor's chambers (which alone cost $800,000 to build) and an Ewok village. Auditions for the Ewoks had actually taken place the previous October, and in the end sixty little people were engaged to play the teddy-like creatures. Among them was Kenny Baker who, as well as playing R2-D2, also got to play the Ewok character Poploo. Also cast as another Ewok named Wicket was twelve-year-old Warwick Davis, who'd first heard about the role on LBC radio. Turning up for an audition at Elstree with his mother, he was hired on the spot, given his two-foot-eleven-inch height. Lucas was immediately taken with Davis, and kept him in mind for some future projects he had in mind.

Filming at Elstree was completed by 4 April, after which cast and crew flew out to Buttercup Valley in Yuma, Arizona, to film the sequences on Jabba the Hutt's Sail Barge, which had taken five months to build. Starting on 12 April, work carried through to 24 April, with everyone having to endure temperatures that often reached 120 degrees farenheit, much to the discomfort of those in robot and monster suits. Despite the far-flung nature of the location, newspaper reporters and hundreds of fans turned up in the desert in the hope of catching a glimpse of the filming. However, given that Lucasfilm had negotiated a six month right of stay on the land from Arizona's Bureau of Land Management,

Chewbacca himself, Peter Mayhew

security was as tight as it could possibly be. Given this extra overhead, the cost of shooting in Yuma eventually came in at a hefty $2.5m

Whilst all this activity was going on, *Star Wars* was re-released for a fourth time in American movie theatres on 10 April, so as to help generate interest in *Jedi* (not that it was needed). Then, in June, the film made its first of many appearances on video. Fans could now actually own their own copy of *Star Wars* and watch it to their heart's content. Later that same year *The Empire Strikes Back* would also re-appear in cinemas, to remind fans what had happened in the installment prior to *Jedi*, whilst on 14 February 1983 a ten-part radio version of *The Empire Strikes Back* was broadcast, featuring Mark Hamill as Luke and John Lithgow (!) as Yoda.

Meanwhile, filming in Yuma complete, everyone moved on to the far more pleasant Crescent City in California on 24 April to film the exterior Endor sequences. Work on the woodlands had actually started in March the previous year, when ferns had been planted so as to be full-grown and ready for shooting the following year. The film's major battle sequence was filmed here, along with the background plates for the Speedbike chase in which Luke and Leia successfully elude Imperial scouts. Luke and Leia would be added to these shots at a later stage by ILM. By 8 May this complex footage was in the can, after which principal photography moved to ILM where blue screen work involving the principals was carried out between 10 May and 14 May.

The film was then turned over to the editors and effects technicians to do their magic. In the case of ILM, they had one hundred more effects shots than *The Empire Strikes Back* to contend with. The final space battle above the part-finished Death Star contained a mind-boggling 67 separate layers (though an oversight in the matting process actually had a Tie Fighter flying through the Millennium Falcon in the sequence!). The model of the Death Star itself was 72 feet long, the making of which took many hours of painstaking work by the team of model-makers.

The effects took eleven months to complete, and were finally finished in April 1983. However, given the busy schedule, John Williams had actually recorded his score for the movie in January and February, often working to a blank screen where effects shots were missing, though he obviously had the storyboards and Lucas's notes to guide him. Using the London Symphony Orchestra, Williams recorded at Abbey Road between 17 January and 10 February. As always, the sessions were recorded by Eric Tomlinson, orchestrated by Herbert W. Spencer and supervised by Lionel Newman. Given the new characters featured in the film, there were a number of new themes added to the score, among them a comical Ewok march, *Parade of the Ewoks*, a sinister *leitmotif* for the Emperor, and a tuba-based theme for Jabba the Hutt. There was also a piece titled *Luke and Leia*.

It was during the scoring of the film, on 27 January, that Lucas finally decided that a title change was needed for the movie. It was not in a Jedi's character to look for revenge, he opined, therefore the film would henceforth be called *Return of the Jedi*. This was a bold move given that posters announcing *Revenge of the Jedi*, featuring Luke and Vader clashing with their lightsabres, had already been circulating, as had tee-shirts and other merchandise (by the end of the nineties, merchandise featuring the *Revenge of the Jedi* logo would be worth fifty times more than that carrying the *Return of the Jedi* logo). Consequently, this teaser poster was replaced by one featuring Luke's hands holding up a lightsabre against a background of stars and planets. This in turn was later replaced with a more elaborate design featuring scenes and characters from the film, among them Han, Luke (lightsabre in hand), Leia, Darth Vader, Lando Calrissian, Jabba the Hutt, a Gamorean Guard and an Ewok. All told it resembled a James Bond poster, given that Leia is seen posing in the revealing bikini costume she wears at the top of the film whilst held prisoner at Jabba's palace.

Return of the Jedi finally opened at cinemas across America on 25 Wednesday May 1983. If anything, the hysteria was even greater than that for *Star Wars* and *The Empire Strikes Back*, with some hardy fans camping out for up to eight days prior to the release, so as to be first in line for the very first showing. Again, box office figures tumbled, the opening day take alone being an industry high of $6.2m. A week later this had risen to an astonishing $45m. By the end of its first run, Jedi scooped a blockbusting $232m in America alone, whilst its worldwide take came in at $348m, putting it behind only *E.T.* and *Star Wars* at the time in the list of top money-making movies. And all this in the face of some healthy competition for a change, including *Flashdance* and *Octopussy*.

Though they failed to influence the box office, the reviews for *Jedi* were more mixed than the ones for *Star Wars* and *Empire*. 'The toys have taken over the toy store,' commented *The Los Angeles Herald Examiner* on the film's surplus of new characters, to which *The New York Times* added, 'Doesn't really end the trilogy as much as it brings it to a dead stop. The film is by far the dimmest adventure of the lot. All of the members of the old *Star Wars* gang are back doing what they've done before, but this time with a certain evident boredom.'

Even the normally positive *Variety* expressed doubts, saying, 'One of the apparent problems is [that] neither the writers nor the principal performers are putting in the same effort.'

Indeed, despite moments of true exhilaration, the movie did feel like a tired and sometimes tiresome wrap-up of preceeding events. Yet some fans hold it as the best in the series, among them, seemingly, critic Roger Ebert, who pronounced that, '*Return of the Jedi* is fun, magnificent fun. The movie is a complete entertainment, a feast for the eyes and a delight for the fancy. It's a little amazing how Lucas and his associates keep topping themselves.'

Though many of the reviews were lukewarm, interest in *Jedi* and *Star Wars* in general was as big as ever. In addition to the toys and novelization, care of James Kahn and Del Ray, there was now also an arcade game from Atari featuring dialogue and music from the movie. *Star Wars* was now very much a part of everyday life no matter where one went.

As to be expected, *Jedi* found itself in line for a number of awards. Oscar-wise it was nominated in six categories, including best music (John Williams), best art direction and set decoration (Norman Reynolds, Fred Hole, James Schoppe, Michael Ford), best sound (Ben Burtt, Gary Summers, Randy Thom, Tony Dawe), best sound effects editing (Ben Burtt) and best visual effects (Richard Edlund, Dennis Muren, Ken Ralston, Phil Tippett). Ultimately, the film went on to win the effects award only, a feat it also repeated at the BAFTAs.

The central *Star Wars* trilogy now completed, Lucas could at last spend more time with his wife and family, enjoying the fruits of his labours. No longer did he have to worry about the exploits of Han, Luke and Leia, et al. However, the real world had a few surprises in store for him.

Mr and Mrs Mark Hamill

17

Back to Reality

In Indiana Jones and the Temple of Doom, the opening Paramount logo segues into a giant gong bearing the same image.

Steven Spielberg, George Lucas and Frank Marshall all make cameo appearances at the airport following the opening chase.

Willie Scott opens the film by singing Cole Porter's Anything Goes *as a portent of things to come.*

The Shanghai nightclub the movie opens in is called Club Obo-Wan.

By the time *Return of the Jedi* was playing in theatres, Lucas had resolved to spend more time with his wife Marcia and their recently-adopted two-year-old daughter Amanda. He intended to have a lengthy vacation and maybe even do some studying. His only real distraction would be the further development of the Skywalker Ranch. Unfortunately, things didn't work out that way, for the constant workload of Lucas's film career had taken its toll on his seemingly-perfect fourteen-year marriage. After much soul searching, it was decided that divorce was the only way forward for the couple, especially as Marcia had been seeing someone else, a worker at the Skywalker Ranch called Tom Rodriguez, whom she later married.

Given the laws in California, Marcia was entitled to half of everything her husband owned in the divorce settlement. To protect the dream of the Skywalker Ranch, a financial settlement was agreed upon, costing Lucas in the region of $50m. Devastated by the split, Lucas eventually filled his emotional void first with a short-lived affair with singer Linda Ronstadt, secondly by adopting two more daughters.

Another casualty of the *Star Wars* phenomenon was Gary Kurtz, who likewise divorced his wife in 1983. He also lost much of his accumulated $10m fortune investing in two movies which failed to set the box office alight: the acclaimed *Dark Crystal* and the derided *Return to Oz*, the latter of which had marked the directorial debut of sound designer Walter Murch. Kurtz filed for bankruptcy in 1985 and, disillusioned with the movie business, went to live in England with his second wife. Another film venture - *Slipstream,* starring Mark Hamill - followed in 1989, but again the film failed to take off at the box office.

If it had originally been Lucas's plan to stay away from the movies and devote more time to Marcia after completing *Jedi*, then his vacation wasn't very long-lived, as the follow-up to *Raiders of the Lost Ark, Indiana Jones and the Temple of Doom*, was already in the pipeline. Originally titled *Indiana Jones and the Temple of Death*, it was to be, at Lucas's behest, much darker in tone than *Raiders*, just as *Empire* had been much darker than *Star Wars*. Instead of being a sequel to *Raiders*, though, it was in fact a prequel. Set in 1935, it follows Indy's attempts to retrieve a sacred Sankara Stone that has been stolen from an impoverished Indian village by the leader of a Khali cult, who intends to re-unite all three stones so as to use their magical powers for his own evil ends.

Indy is accompanied on this quest by an American singer called Willie Scott, whom he has rescued from the clutches of her ganglord escort, Lao Che, in a Shaghai nightclub fracas. Also along for the ride is Indy's eleven-year-old sidekick Short Round. As to be expected, the trio discover themselves in all manner of tight corners, chiefly in the bowels of the Palace of Pankot where they find themselves at the mercy of the Khali cult. The many action highlights in the movie included an opening nightclub fight, a jump from a stalling plane in an inflatable liferaft, a getaway in a minecar and a standoff on a collapsing rope bridge, not to mention an encounter with a million creepy crawlies.

Having worked out the basics of the story, Lucas, as was now usual, handed over the scripting duties, this time to his friends Gloria Katz and Willard Huyck, who worked against the clock so that Steven Spielberg would be able to fit shooting the movie into his increasingly busy schedule. A few minor re-writes aside, they completed their work in just four months. The script was then storyboarded by Ed Verreaux, Joe Johnston, Andrew G. Probert and Stanley Fleming, who worked from Spielberg's customary doodles.

Budgeted at $27.5m, the movie began shooting on 18 April 1983, with Harrison Ford back in Indy's trademark Fedora. Also in the cast was Spielberg's soon-to-be second wife Kate Capshaw as dizzy nightclub singer Willie Scott, Roshan Seth as Chattar Lal, the devious Prime Minister to His Highness the Maharajah of Pankot, Amrish Puri as villain-in-chief Mola Ram, and Roy Chiao as the cunning Lao Che. To play Indy's savvy sidekick Short Round (named after Katz and Huyck's dog), casting director Mike Fenton and his associates auditioned hundreds of children in London, New York, San Francisco, Los Angeles, Honolulu and Vancouver, eventually settling on Ke Huy Quan, a Vietnamese-born boy who had been living in America since the age of six. *Temple of Doom* would be his break, which he'd later follow up with roles in *The Goonies* (produced by Spielberg's Amblin Entertainment company) and the television series *Together We Stand*.

Also in the cast was a heavily-disguised Dan Aykroyd as airport official Weber, whom Indy, Willie and Short Round encounter at Nang Tao airport in their bid to escape Lao Che. Similarly disguised are Spielberg, Lucas and Frank Marshall, who supposedly make gag cameos as refugees at the airport. Another familar face onboard was Pat Roach, who returned for his customary fist fight with Indy, this time as the Chief Guard in the underground temple.

Behind the cameras were many of the usual suspects, among them Frank Marshall, who co-executive produced the film with Lucas, Robert Watts, who was producing, Kathleen Kennedy, who was the film's associate producer, and Douglas Slocombe, who was again in charge of photography. Michael Moore again headed the second unit, whilst Vic Armstrong and Glenn Randall were in charge of the stunts. Marshall and Randall also contributed to the direction of certain second unit sequences.

As is often the case with movies, the film wasn't shot in the order of the script. The first sequence filmed was actually the last scene in the movie, when Indy, Willie and Short Round return to the village in triumph with the stolen stone and the children who have been kidnapped by the cult (echoes of *Chitty Chitty*

116

Bang Bang there). This was done so that the village, revived by its good fortune in this sequence, could then be partially destroyed to show its despair when Indy first arrives there and learns of its people's troubles.

These scenes, along with many of the other exteriors, were all shot in Sri Lanka and Macau, as the Indian government had objected to elements in the *Temple of Doom* script. Macau also stood in for the streets of Shanghai. As usual, the interiors were shot at Elstree, where the lavish rooms of the Pankot Palace were created by production designer Elliot Scott. A newcomer to the Lucas/Spielberg camp, Scott had worked on such fantasy favourites as *Tom Thumb*, *Children of the Damned*, *The Warlords of Atlantis* and *Dragonslayer*, though it had probably been his work for *Arabian Adventure* that made him the ideal candidate to bring the world of thirties Shanghai and India to life.

The sacrificial altar of the cult was also built at Elstree, along with many of the booby-trapped corridors Indy, Willie and Short Round find themselves stuck in. One of the most memorable scenes in the movie was shot here, which involves Willie trying to rescue Indy and Short Round from being crushed to death in a chamber of descending spikes. However, to do this, she has make her way down a corridor literally alive with bugs. 250,000 cockroaches and other nasties were specially bred for this scene, which proved a nightmare for Kate Capshaw to film, given her fear of creepy crawlies.

The last scene to be shot at Elstree was actually the opening musical sequence, a Busby Berkeley spoof in which Willie sings Cole Porter's *Anything Goes* - in Mandarin, no less! - over the opening titles, accompanied by a chorus of beauties choreographed in Berkeley style by Danny Daniels. Then it was off to America to film the bluescreen work at ILM, plus some pick-up shots at Hamilton Air Force Base. All in all, the main shoot would take five months to complete, wrapping on 8 September 1983. However, it would take a further four months to realise the film's elaborate effects, with the ILM team devoting most of their time to the mine chase sequence towards the end of the movie.

Post production was finally completed on 24 March 1984, including Ben Burtt's sound mix and the addition of John Williams' score, which was this time recorded at the MGM Music Scoring Stage in Culver City California, using established session musicians as opposed to The London Symphony Orchestra. The film was then released on 23 May 1984, accompanied by a colourful poster whose tag line read, 'If adventure has a name, it must be Indiana Jones.' Audiences agreed to the tune of $231m at the American box office alone.

The film, however, was not without controversy. Its scenes of violence were deemed too strong for younger audiences, prompting the MPAA to create a new rating for the film, PG-13. The violent nature of the movie also came in for criticisim in the press. 'An astonishing violation of the trust people have in Spielberg's and Lucas's essentially good-natured approach to movies primarily intended for kids,' commented *People* magazine. *Variety* was also critical, saying, 'Steven Spielberg has packed even more thrills and chills into this follow-up than he did into the earlier pic, but to exhausting and numbing effect... Capshaw, who looks fetching in her native attire, has unfortunately been asked to react hysterically to everything that happens to her.' *Newsweek* also found the film something of an assault on the senses, adding, 'Spielberg has gone to such lengths to avoid boredom that he has leaped squarely into the opposite trap: this movie has such unrelenting action that it jackhammers you into a punch-drunk stupor.'

The film does certainly move fast, thanks to Michael Kahn's slick editing. Cinematically, the film is also a *tour de force* of imaginative directorial touches. However, the relentless pace and John Williams's emphatic score do leave one somewhat wrung out by the end. Still, audiences flocked to the film, and many critics found much to admire in it. 'One of the most sheerly pleasurable comedies ever made,' wrote Pauline Kael, to which the ever-enthusiastic Roger Ebert added, 'It's a rollercoaster ride, a visual extravaganza, a technical triumph, and a whole lot of fun. Not so much a sequel as an equal.'

As was now becoming a habit with all of Lucas's films, *Temple of Doom* found itself in line for a number of awards. Oscar-wise it was nominated for best music (John Williams) and best visual effects (Dennis Muren, Michael McAlister, Lorne Peterson, George Gibbs), going on to win the latter, an achievement it repeated at the BAFTAs. Surprisingly, the film failed to earn any Oscar nominations for Elliot Scott's production design, Michael Kahn's editing nor for Anthony Powell's excellent costume design.

With such an enormous box office take, this barely seemed to matter, though. Lucas's private life may have been going through a rough patch. His professional standing was as secure as ever, however.

18

The Return of the Ewoks

In The Ewok Adventure: Caravan of Courage, *Winnie the Pooh can be spotted sitting in a tree in one of the film's matte paintings.*

In the opening sequence, Howard the Duck is reading a copy of Playduck. *On the floor lies copies of* Fowl *and* Rolling Egg.

Concept designer Brian Froud's baby son Toby plays Toby in Labyrinth.

Despite a few cynical comments from various quarters about the Ewoks in *Return of the Jedi*, the cuddly creatures proved irresistible with children (as no doubt intended). Consequently, Lucas was persuaded to resurrect the creatures for television. The result was the 1984 tele-movie *The Ewok Adventure: Caravan of Courage*, which Lucas provided the story outline for and also executive produced.

The treatment, which was subsequently turned into a full-length script by Bob

Carrau, centres round the Towani family, who crash-land their star cruiser on Endor. Whilst the parents, Jeremitt and Catarine, go off to seek help, the kids, Mace and Cindel, are left behind to await their return. However, when mom and pop fail to come back, the two kids hike off by themselves, encountering the Ewoks along the way, as well as a handful of strange creatures.

Wicket, the Ewok featured in *Jedi*, returned as the central Ewok character and was again played by the diminutive Warwick Davis, whilst the roles of the two children were played by newcomers Aubree Miller and Eric Walker. Guy Boyd and Fionnula Flanagan were along for the ride as the parents.

An expensive production by normal television standards, the film benefited from solid production design by Joe Johnston, who had graduated from storyboarding and effects work on previous Lucas movies. To direct, Lucas brought back John Korty, who also photographed the film. Korty's previous Lucas film, *Twice Upon a Time*, may have met with box office indifference, but that wasn't to be the case with *The Ewok Adventure*, which proved highly popular when aired over Thanksgiving in 1984. So much so that it was released theatrically outside America to healthy box office returns.

Produced by Tom Smith, formerly ILM's general manager, *The Ewok Adventure* shot on location in North California and Marin County in June 1984. Michael Pangrazio then supervised the film's effects work, which involved the addition of matte paintings and blue screen shots. There was even a little stop motion animation thrown in for good measure care of Jon Berg and Phil Tippett, who animated a creature called a Gorax for the film. Capped off with a score by Peter Bernstein, who made use of several of John Williams's themes, the film was generally well received. In fact it went on to win an Emmy for best effects, plus a nomination for outstanding children's programming. The International Television Movie Festival also gave it an award for best children's production, along with a Gold Medal for best effects.

Inevitably, a sequel was called for, which duly arrived the following year. Called *Ewoks: The Battle for Endor*, it followed the adventures of Cindel and Wicket, who flee the Ewok village when it is invaded King Terak and his followers. In the skirmish, Cindel's parents and brother are killed, leaving the young girl an orphan and dependant on Wicket for help. Encounters with a wicked witch called Charal and an Obi-Wan Kenobi-like hermit follow before the inevitable happy(ish) ending.

As always, Lucas executive produced and provided the story, which this time was scripted and directed by Jim and Ken Wheat, with Joe Johnston returning

Walter Murch, director of *Return to Oz*, pictured with artwork prepared for the movie

as production designer (with Harley Jessup), Peter Bernstein as composer and Tom Smith as producer. New to the cast were Wilford Brimley as the hermit and Sian Phillips as Charal, whilst Aubree Miller returned as Cindel and Warwick Davis as Wicket.

Again, the movie was released theatrically outside the States. It also won an Emmy for best special effects and a nomination for outstanding children's programming and sound mixing for a miniseries or special. As well as conquering the big screen, it now looked as if Lucas was doing the same thing on the small screen. In fact so popular did the two Ewok tele-movies prove, further spin-offs followed. The first of these was *The Ewoks and Droids Adventure Hour*, an animated series which contained segments featuring the adventures of R2-D2, C-3PO (voiced by Anthony Daniels) and the Ewoks. Made by Nelvana Productions in association with Lucasfilm, the series was broadcast in 1985 and proved popular enough to spawn a second series, now simply titled *Ewoks*, which aired in 1986. Budgeted at $500,000 per episode,

121

they were made in Canada, where they were supervised by Miki Herman, who had been the production manager on *Return of the Jedi*.

1986 also saw the broadcast of another Nelvana/Lucasfilm animated production. This was *The Great Heep*, an hour-long programme scripted by sound designer Ben Burtt, which sees R2-D2 and C-3PO (voiced by Daniels) off to the planet Biitu to take up duties with their new master, an explorer called Mungo Boabab. Inevitably, things don't quite go according to plan, and the two droids discover that Biitu has been taken over by a giant robot known as The Great Heep, whom they help to defeat with the help of Boabab, a young boy called Fidge and another droid, KT-10, whom R2-D2 falls in love with!

Ben Burtt, as well as writing *The Great Heep*, also designed its sound, whilst Joe Johnston designed the look of the programme, including The Great Heep itself. Directed by Clive Smith, with songs by Derek Holt and Stewart Copeland, the one-hour special proved popular with its intended audience.

Back on the big screen, Lucas involved himself peripherally in a number of projects, among them *Return to Oz*, for which he took no screen credit. This movie, which saw a psychologically traumatised Dorothy (newcomer Fairuza Balk) return to Oz for further adventures, marked the directorial debut of sound designer and editor Walter Murch. A big budget affair involving complex make-up, sets (care of Norman Reynolds) and effects, it was having production problems which Murch asked Lucas's advice over, along with that of Robert Watts, both of whom are 'thanked' in the end credits for their efforts. Whatever behind-the-scenes problems the movie had, it was ultimately its onscreen deficiencies that kept audiences away. Though technically adroit, it was unnecessarily melancholy in comparison to its colourful, upbeat 1939 predecessor. A misguided venture, it was ironically executive produced by Gary Kurtz, who surely must have bridled at Lucas's attempts to 'rescue' the movie, which was released to an unenthusiastic world in 1985.

1985 also saw the release of *Mishima*, which Lucas co-executive produced with Francis Ford Coppola. A biopic about the Japanese writer Yukio Mishima, it was directed by Paul Schrader from a script by Schrader and his brother Leonard. Very much an arthouse production, it did little business in America, but garnered some respectable reviews, though critic Leslie Halliwell's comment that the film was, 'half a work of art and half an utter waste of other people's money,' perhaps best summed up its aims and failures.

Lucas also involved himself in *Latino*, a 1986 release which was a Lucasfilm 'presentation'. Written and directed by Lucas's friend, acclaimed

Ken Ogata stars in *Mishima*

cinematographer Haskel Wexler, the movie was a political drama about America's involvement in Nicaragua, where the movie was actually shot. Centering on the Contras' fight against the Sandinistas, the movie starred Robert Beltran and, like Wexler's 1969 film *Medium Cool*, had a strong documentary flavour to it. Lucas offered advice on the script and editing, just as Wexler had advised Lucas during the filming of *American Graffiti*. Lucas was merely helping his friend and returning a favour. The name of Lucasfilm on the credits no doubt also helped to secure the movie a release, though like *Mishima*, it was too specialised for mainstream success.

1986 was proving to be a busy year for Lucas, for it also saw the release of two big budget movies he was directly involved in. The first of these was *Labyrinth*, a fantasy about teenage girl whose baby step-brother is kidnapped by the King of the Goblins whilst her parents are away for the evening. To get the child back, the girl must pass through an elaborate labyrinth, where she encounters all manner of weird creatures, including a helpful giant called Ludo.

Scripted by *Monty Python* star Terry Jones from a story by Muppetmeister Jim Henson and his friend Dennis Less, *Labyrinth* was to be a fantasy spectacular in the manner of Henson's previous *Dark Crystal*. As usual, Lucas assumed his usual role as executive producer (with David Lazer), whilst onboard to bring the story to life were producer Eric Rattray, production designer Elliot Scott, conceptual designer Brian Fround and effects technician George Gibbs. In front of the camera, pop music legend David Bowie starred as the King of the Goblins (he also provided several songs for the movie), whilst Jennifer Connelly, whose face was becoming familiar after appearances in *Once Upon a Time in Ameica* and *Phenomena* (aka *Creepers*), played the girl Sarah. Brian Froud's son Toby played the baby.

Filming began in England at Elstree in April 1985. Lucas tried to downplay his role in the movie, commenting that it was Henson's production - he had just contributed a few ideas. Yet despite the best intentions of all concerned, *Labyrinth*, though often visually arresting thanks to Elliot Scott's design work, never really took off as a story. Despite its expense, it was charmless and never really generated any sympathy for its young heroine's plight. Said *Variety* of the production, 'An array of bizarre creatures and David Bowie can't even save *Labyrinth* from being a crashing bore. Characters created by Jim Henson and his team become annoying rather than endearing. What is even more disappointing is the failure of the film on a story level [which] soon loses its way and never comes close to archetypal myths and fears of great fairy tales. Instead it's an unconvincing coming of age saga.'

The dream team of Lucas and Henson had failed to pull off what should have been a dead cert. Like *Variety*, audiences were similarly unimpressed by the movie, which did only reasonable box office, despite the extra publicity push of the Prince and Princess of Wales seeing the movie at a gala London screening. However, if audiences had been unimpressed by *Labyrinth*, they were downright hostile towards Lucas's next movie, the lamentable *Howard the Duck*.

Following their work as scriptwriters on *American Graffiti* and *Indiana Jones and the Temple of Doom*, Lucas gave his friends Willard Huyck and Gloria Katz a shot at the big time by allowing them to write, direct (Huyck) and produce (Katz, with Robert Latham Brown) his next movie, which was based on the Steve Gerber comic strip about a duck from another world who finds himself beamed across the universe to Cleveland where he becomes something of a superhero.

Part of Marvel's *Manthing* comic series of 1973, the original *Howard the Duck* comic strip revelled in weird storylines, including one which had barbarian warriors leaping out of peanut butter jars! Marvel hated the character and ordered that he be killed off, yet readers liked him. He wasn't a superhero, just an ordinary guy, albeit a duck. As a consequence, Marvel faced a lawsuit from Disney, who claimed Howard looked too much like Donald. Negotiations thus followed between 1977 and 1983, the earth-shattering conclusion of which was that Howard should always wear trousers, presumably so as not to confuse fans. This wasn't the only row over the character, though. Marvel claimed that it was the company, and not Gerber, who owned the character. Consequently, Gerber left the company, and though the comic strip continued, it lacked its former sparkle, and was wound down in 1981.

Yet fans remained loyal to the character, among them Lucas, who showed the comic strips to Willard Huyck and Gloria Katz. Deciding the character might adapt to movies, Lucas attempted to get the rights. It was a complicated process, however, as Universal owned part of the package, which also included the rights to *The Incredible Hulk*. The process took an astonishing ten years to complete, after which Lucas and Universal teamed up to bring the movie to the big screen (apparently, Universal's original idea had been to turn *Howard the Duck* into a weekly television show).

Budgeted at $50m, *Howard the Duck* was slightly modified for the big screen, given the character's propensity for crude language in the original strip. Katz and Huyck thus made him a more sensitive and responsive character in their script, an approach which surprisingly won the respect of Steve Gerber. As did the realisation of Howard himself. Designed by Nilo Rodis-Jamero and built by ILM, the character had an animatronic head which allowed him to talk without strings and wires. At the end of the day, though, Howard was still a midget in a duck suit (eight of them are credited with the part: Ed Gale, Chip Zien, Tim Rose, Steve Sleap, Peter Baird, Mary Wells, Lisa Sturz and Jordan Prentice).

Among the humans in the cast were Lea Thompson, familiar from *Back to the Future*, who plays rock singer Beverly Switzler, whom Howard rescues from some punks. She then offers to help Howard find his way back home, avoiding the authorities along the way, who naturally want to capture Howard for their own nefarious ends. Also along for the ride was Tim Robbins, who played Switzler's friend Phil Blumburtt, and Jeffrey Jones as the evil Doctor Jenning.

The movie was a non-starter from the word go, even though bolstered by a Thomas Dolby songscore. Despite some good effects work (including a stop-motion monster created and animated by Phil Tippett) and a few goodish visual gags (on Howard's home planet, he is shown in his apartment reading *Playduck* and *Rolling Egg*, whilst drinking Birdweiser beer), the film was misconceieved from the outset. Its failure at the box office did Lucas's reputation no good at all. Nor did the reviews. Said *Variety*, 'Scripters have taken the cigar chompin', beer drinkin' Marvel Comics character and turned him into a wide-eyed, cutesy, midget-sized extraterrestrial.' *People Weekly* agreed, commenting, 'Watching an actor waddle around in the unimpressive costume, you don't know if you're at a movie or a shopping mall opening,' to which *Time* added, 'Moviegoers who are in search of a porno Zoo Parade may enjoy the bedroom tryst in which Howard's human sweetie (Lea Thompson) discovers a condom in his wallet, snuggles up and asks, "You think I might find love in the animal kingdom?" More fastidious viewers are advised to purchase a *Daffy Duck* videocassette.'

With reviews like that, audiences stayed away in droves. Universal tried to repair the damage, cutting some of the movie's more risque touches. It even retitled the film for overseas release, calling it *Howard: A New Breed of Hero*. Nothing worked though, and the movie managed to recoup just $15m of its whopping $50m outlay. A financial disaster of some significance, its failure cost Universal executive Frank Price his job. Universal's shares also took a dive as a consequence, whilst Lucas's reputation was severely tarnished.

Not all was doom and gloom in 1986. The previous year Lucas had been approached by Disney who wanted a movie to launch their 3D Magic Eye Theatre for their theme parks in California and Florida. Lucas came up with *Captain Eo*, a seventeen minute fantasy adventure in which the captain of a spaceship lands on a planet ruled by an evil queen. To play the part of Eo, Lucas managed to persuade singing superstar Michael Jackson to take on the role, whilst Anjelica Huston played the queen.

Written and executive produced by Lucas, the $10m movie was directed by Francis Ford Coppola, with his regular cinematographer Vittorio Storaro in charge of the 3D photography, which was achieved by using two perfectly synchronised 65mm cameras with polarising filters over their lenses, which were set just two-and-a-half inches apart (the same as human eyes). Meannwhile, the music for *Captain Eo* was provided by Jackson himself (who

The source material: Steve Gerber's *Howard The Duck* © Marvel Comics also contributed to the story), whilst the design was by John Napier and Geoffrey Kirkland. Rusty Lemorande was the overall producer. As ever, ILM were in charge of the effects, which included a motion-controlled spaceship, matte paintings and stop-motion animation, all of which was overseen by Disney's effects supervisor Harrison Ellenshaw, best known for his work on Disney's *Star Wars* clone *The Black Hole*.

An instant hit with the theme park crowds, the film ran for several years, though more cynical audience members found some of the film's robots and muppet-style creatures a little too twee for comfort, among them being Fuzzball, an orange-haired flying monkey, Geex, a two-headed creature with one right foot and two left feet, Major Domo, a robot who uses his metal body as drums, and Minor Domo, whose metallic body forms a synthesiser. All of these were naturally merchandized and available to buy in shops in the parks.

Lucas's involvement with Disney didn't end with *Captain Eo*. In 1986 he agreed to collaborate with the company to create a Star Tours ride, which was launched during a sixty-hour non-stop party between 9 and 11 January 1987. In the four-and-a-half minute simulator ride, holidaymakers board a Star Speeder 3000 shuttle for a tour of the galaxy. Given that there is a rookie droid at the controls, the ride takes some unexpected twists and turns before returning to base. ILM provided the effects needed for the ride, which were supervised by Dennis Muren and Dave Carson, who had the shuttle shooting through an ice tunnel and over a Death Star.

With animatronics on show in the queuing areas, including C-3PO as voiced by Anthony Daniels, the ride proved another hit with theme park patrons, who were herded through the ride at a rate of 1,600 per hour via four identical shuttles. Naturally, when they emerged from their experience, there was plenty of merchandising on sale in the shops directly by the ride's exit.

Then in 1987 came the tenth anniversary of *Star Wars*, which was naturally re-released to mark the event. By this time interest in the series was inevitably waning. The *Return of the Jedi* weekly magazine had already folded, as had the *Star Wars* Fan Club in the UK. The tenth anniversary was something else, though, and it not only renewed interest in the series, but also raised the question as to whether Lucas would ever continue the saga or not. Lucas supported the anniversary celebrations, and at a rare convention appearance he told an expectant audience that any follow-ups were not yet imminent. Indeed, he had a few other ideas to bring to the big screen first.

19
Thinking Small

In Willow, *the two-headed moat monster was christened the Eborsisk by the ILM effects crew, after film critics Gene Sisker and Roger Ebert, though no mention of this is made in the actual film.*

Bad guy Kael is named after film critic Pauline Kael.

The name of The High Aldwin (played by Billy Bart) means Old One.

A car in Tucker *carries the registration GIO, which was the name of Francis Ford Coppola's son who died during the film's production, hence the dedication, 'For Gio... who loved cars'.*

As he had done on *Latino* and *Mishima*, Lucas used his influence to get Godfrey Reggio's follow-up to his 1983 movie *Koyaanisqatsi* off the ground. Released in 1988, this visual tour de force went by the title *Powaqqatsi*, and provided some eye-catching visuals of the Third World, though like *Latino* and *Mishima*, it was strictly an arthouse affair.

Meanwhile, of Lucas's personal projects, next in line was the fantasy adventure *Willow*. Lucas had originally wanted to make *The Lord of the Rings*, but the rights belonged to Saul Zaentz, the producer of the 1978 Ralph Bakshi-directed cartoon version, and he wasn't about to relinquish them, his longterm intention being to make a live action version of the story at some stage. Consequently, Lucas used *The Lord of the Rings* as the jumping off point for *Willow*, just as *Flash Gordon* had been his inspiration for *Star Wars*.

Like *Star Wars*, *Willow* is deeply rooted in Lucas's love of mythology, its story, by Lucas himself, centring round the discovery of a baby girl called Elora who had been hidden in a village of Newlyns (for which read little people). The child's nurse has hidden the baby becase she believes her to be the successor to the evil Queen Bavmorda, who has ordered that all baby girls be slain. The Newlyn who finds Elora, Willow Ufgood, determines on protecting her and returning her so that she can achieve her destiny. Thus an incredible journey, fraught with danger at every turn, begins.

Naturally, Willow doesn't make this journey alone. Along the way he is joined by Madmartigan, a maverick swordsman, and a feisty maiden called Sorsha who turns out to be Queen Bavmorda's daughter, both of whom help conquer Bavmorda. There is also assistance in the form of a sorceress called Raziel and the wise High Aldwin, and further hindrance in the shape of General Kael (named after critic Pauline Kael). There is also a giant two-headed monster which the effects team at ILM Christened the Eborsisk (after critics Roger Ebert and Gene Siskel).

To flesh out his story, Lucas hired Bob Dolman, who was then working on the sit-com *WKRP in Cincinnati*. To direct he only ever really had his former *American Graffiti* star Ron Howard in mind, whose directorial career had by now taken in *Grand Theft Auto*, *Night Shift*, *Splash*, *Cocoon* and *Gung Ho*, of which both *Splash* and *Cocoon* had been huge box office hits. Other behind-the-scenes personnel onboard included producer Nigel Wooll, cinematographer Adrian Biddle (*Aliens*, *The Princess Bride*), production designer Allan Cameron (*Aliens*), sound designer Ben Burtt and ILM technicians Dennis Muren, Michael J. McAlister and Phil Tippett. As usual, Lucas executive produced. In front of the cameras, Warwick Davis finally got his big moment as Willow, supported by Val Kilmer as Madmartigan, Joanne Whalley as Sorsha, Jean Marsh as Bavmorda, Patricia Hayes as Raziel, Billy Barty as The High Aldwin and Pat Roach as General Kael. Twins Ruth and Kate Greenfield provided the close-ups of Elora, whilst Kenny Baker and his cabaret partner Jack Purvis also popped up in one of the Newlyn scenes. Another hundred or so little people were also cast as Newlyns, no doubt grateful to be acting in something other than a *Snow White* pantomime.

Story-wise, *Willow* wasn't that far removed from *Star Wars*. Madmartigan was a thinly disguised Han Solo, Willow was a diminutive Luke Skywalker, Sorsha was Leia, General Kael Darth Vader and both The High Aldwin and Raziel had echoes of Yoda. There were also elements of Lucas's beloved Samurai movies thrown in for good measure, most notably in the costumes by Barbara Lane.

Budgeted at $40m, *Willow* began filming on 27 April 1987, and during its lengthy six month shoot the production visited Snowdonia in Wales and the Queenstown mountain district in New Zealand, the spectacular scenery of which added immeasurably to the film's visual appeal. As always, all the interiors were shot at Elstree. Whilst all this was going on, back in Marin County the ILM technicians were excelling themselves, providing many magical effects sequences, including Raziel's seamless transformation from a goat to human form via several different animals. They also had to contend with two minor characters, Rool and Franjean (Kevin Pollack and Rick Overton) who are just nine inches tall, yet play a vital part in several action sequences.

Having been edited by Daniel Hanley and Michael Hill, and scored by James Horner, *Willow* was ready for screening at Cannes in May 1988, where it was the festival's official closing film. It was released in America soon after on 20 May, and though it did reasonable box office business, it didn't exactly set the world alight, being overshadowed by *Who Framed Roger Rabbit?*, which proved to be the year's big hit. Consequently, any plans for a sequel to *Willow* were quietly shelved by Lucas.

Though well made and enjoyable in itself, the movie's problem seemed to be the familiarity of its characters and themes, which several critics picked up on, most notably *Variety*, which commented, '*Willow*... is a sort of 10th century *Star Wars* tossed together with a plethora of elements taken from numerous classic fables. Ron Howard directed, but only Lucasness shows up on the screen, particularly towards the end when the special effects start to come on at full bore. It's not surprising that the overall flavour of the production looks familiar.'

Despite its lukewarm reception, *Willow* did nevertheless earn a couple of Academy Award nominations for best special effects (Dennis Muren, Phil Tippett, Michael J. McAlister) and best sound effects editing (Ben Burtt), both of which it lost to *Who Framed Roger Rabbit?*

1988 also saw the release of another film executive produced by Lucas. This was *Tucker: The Man and His Dream*, Francis Ford Coppola's biopic of Preston Tucker, a car designer who, after World War Two, attempted to outdo Ford, Chrysler and General Motors by manufacturing his own vehicles. Given the stiff competition, it was inevitable that he would fail. Tucker only managed to produce 50 cars, most of which, now highly prized, are still running today (Coppola himself owns two, Lucas one).

Perhaps because of its downbeat conclusion, the film failed to find an audience. Nevertheless, it remains one of Coppola's slickest films. Produced by Fred Fuchs and former casting director Fred Roos, the film was photographed by Vittorio Storaro, designed by Dean Tavoularis and had a snappy score by Joe Jackson. Jeff Bridges played the personable Preston Tucker, supported by his father Lloyd Bridges, Joan Allen, Dean Stockwell, Frederic Forrest and Martin Landau.

The film was nominated for a handful of Academy Awards, including best supporting actor (Martin Landau), best costume design (Milena Canonero) and best art direction and set decoration (Dean Tavoularis, Armin Ganz). Though it failed to win Oscars, it did take home a BAFTA for production design (Dean Tavoularis), a New York Film Critics' Circle Award for best supporting actor (Dean Stockwell), a National Society of Film Critics' Award for best supporting actor (Dean Stockwell) and a Golden Globe for best supporting actor (Martin Landau).

A film that Lucas was involved in that did make money in 1988 was the animated feature *The Land Before Time*. The story of a baby brontosaurus called Littlefoot, it had various parallels with Disney's *Bambi*, in that Littlefoot and his mother have to leave their pastures when they start drying up to search for new sources of food. Unfortunaately, Littlefoot's mother is killed in an earthquake on the journey, leaving the little tyke to fend for himself in a hostile world. The film was directed by former Disney animator Don Bluth, who had had success both with The *Secret of NIMH* and *An American Tail*, the latter of which had been executive produced by Steven Spielberg, who now asked Lucas to join him, Frank Marshall and Kathleen Kennedy on *The Land Before Time* in the same capacity.

Lucas couldn't resist the offer, and helped to contribute ideas to the film's story. The results were stickily sweet and sentimental when they weren't thin, but the film was visually attractive and appealed mightily to youngsters and some less cynical adults. 'Sure, kids like dinosaurs, but beyond that, [the] premise doesn't find far to go,' commented *Variety*. Nevertheless, the movie provoked a string of made-for-video sequels, including *The Land Before Time II: The Great Valley Adventure*, *The Land Before Time III: The Time of the Great Giving*, and *The Land Before Time IV*.

The late eighties had proved to be something of a hit and miss period for Lucas. However, if *Howard the Duck* and *Willow* hadn't exactly set the box office alight, then his last major film of the decade would set matters to rights.

20
Back to the Hat

The opening Paramount logo segues into a giant rock of similar shape.

Reference is made to the Ark of the Covenant,
which Indy had discovered on his previous adventure
*(*Temple of Doom *was a prequel to* Raiders*).*

We learn that Indy/Harrison Ford got his trademark scar on his chin
by mis-handling a whip in the opening serquence.

The wife of Walter Donovan (Julian Glover) is played by the actor's
wife, who is billed as Mrs Glover.

1989 started off well for Lucas, for *Star Wars* was among the first 25 titles placed on the US National Film Registry by the Library of Congress's Film Preservation Board. *Star Wars* was now officially recognized as a film of cultural, historical and aesthetic value.

Even better news for Indiana Jones fans was the release of the third movie in the series, *Indiana Jones and the Last Crusade*. Work had actually started on

134

the movie over two years earlier when ideas about what form the story for this episode would take. Lucas first tinkered with the idea of a haunted house scenario, but this was quickly discarded given the restrictions it would place on the action. Steven Spielberg, who would be directing again, also had strong reservations about this idea given that he had already produced (and some say directed) *Poltergeist*. Another story about an African Monkey King was also seriously considered, so much so that some initial location scouting was undertaken in Africa by Lucas, Frank Marshall and Kathleen Kennedy. A script by Chris Columbus (who had already written *Gremlins*, *The Goonies* and *The Young Sherlock Holmes* for Spielberg's Amblin company, and would later go on to direct *Home Alone*, *Home Alone 2* and *Mrs Doubtfire*) was even commissioned. Ultimately, though, it was discarded in favour of a story centred round the search for the Holy Grail.

Lucas thus began to work on the story along with writer Menno Meyjes, who had been nominated for an Academy Award for his screenplay for Spielberg's *The Color Purple*. This was then taken up by another writer, Jeffrey Boam (who'd penned *The Dead Zone*, *The Lost Boys* and *Innerspace*), who was instructed to make the script more akin to the light-hearted nature of *Raiders of the Lost Ark*, rather than the dark and menacing tone of *Indiana Jones and the Temple of Doom*. Consequently, Denholm Elliott was brought back as Marcus Brody, and John Rhys Davies as Sallah, both of whom join Indy in his adventures, adding some welcome humour to the proceedings.

The main thrust of the screenplay, which was delivered in October 1987, is Indy's search for the Holy Grail, a quest in which he is joined by his father, Dr Henry Jones, whose lifelong goal its discovery has been. Naturally, the Nazis are also after the Grail, so the chase is on to see who reaches it first. The story is thus basically a rehash of *Raiders*.

To play Indy's father, Spielberg had the inspired idea of casting James Bond himself, Sean Connery. The onscreen rapport between him and Ford produced some excellent banter and also added an extra dimension to the proceedings, especially during the film's climactic scenes when Jones Sr lies dying, his life dependent on his son's discovery of the Grail, whose magical properties will save him. For a time, Connery dithered whether or not to play Jones Sr and instead almost signed to play Spock's half-brother Sybok in *Star Trek V: The Final Frontier*. Luckily he signed up for *Last Crusade*, which is just as well, for *Star Trek V* was one of the biggest flops of the summer '89 season.

Also part of *Last Crusade's* story is the beautiful but duplicitous Dr Elsa

Schneider (played by newcomer Alison Doody), who uses her sexual wiles on both Jones Jr and Sr to extract information about the whereabouts of the Grail for the Nazis. Equally duplicitous is socialite Walter Donovan (Julian Glover), who also has an interest in the Grail's discovery.

As always, the thrills came thick and fast, from an opening sequence featuring the young Indiana Jones (played by River Phoenix), who attempts to prevent a group of tomb-raiders from making off with The Cross of Coronado, through to the climax, in which Indy has to survive a series of elborate deathtraps so as to get to the Grail, which is guarded by a 700-year-old Arthurian knight (played by Robert Eddison). Along the way there are sequences on a storm-drenched trawler, onboard a dirigible, in rat-infested catacombs (echoes of *Temple of Doom's* bug sequence), on a speeding tank, and in a Nazi-occupied castle and on a Venice canal (actually shot on the River Thames in London). We also learn where Indy got his fear of snakes from, and how he got the scar on his chin. There is even an encounter with Adolf Hitler himself (which was Spielberg's idea), whilst the film ends with a take on one of the cinema's greatest visual clichés - our hero rides off into the sunset.

Some changes were made to the script during pre-production. The opening featuring the young Indy was originally to have centred round the older Indy's search for a rare Inca artefact in the southwest. This involved a fight in a bar with a group of bandits. The scene was dropped because it played too much like a western rather than an Indiana Jones adventure.

Filming on *Last Crusade*, which was budgeted at $44m, began in May 1988 and took in locations in Spain (covering for Austria), Jordan, Venice, New Mexico, Utah and Colorado. As ever, the film's interiors were shot at Elstree. Behind the cameras was the by now familiar crew of producer Robert Watts, cinematographer Douglas Slocombe, editor Michael Kahn and production designer Elliot Scott, whilst the effects were in the capable hands of ILM's Michael J. McAlister and George Gibbs. Frank Marshall, who co-exectuive produced with Lucas, also handled the second unit sequences with Michael Moore, whilst Vic Armstrong was again in charge of the breathtaking stunts. The music was naturally by John Williams, who this time curiously eschewed The London Symphony Orchestra in favour of a standard Hollywood session orchestra.

A box office smash the world over upon its release, *Last Crusade* also garnered some respectable reviews. Said *Variety*, 'This literate adventure should entertain and enlighten kids and adults alike... The Harrison Ford-Sean

136

Connery father-and-son team gives *Last Crusade* unexpected emotional depth, reminding us that real film magic is not in special effects.' This time Pauline Kael agreed, commenting, 'It makes you want to cheer - you leave the theatre laughing at your own excitement.'

As to be expected, the film was in line for some Academy Award nominations, this time for best score (John Williams), best sound (Ben Burtt, Gary Summers, Shawn Murphy, Tony Dawe) and best sound effects editing (Ben Burtt, Richard Hymns), the latter of which it won. Thus following the commercial disappointments of both *Willow* and *Howard the Duck*, Lucas prepared to enter the nineties with his credibility restored. The question was, now that the *Indiana Jones* trilogy was completed, what would be next in line?

21

Dusting Down the Past

Radioland Murders is dedicated to actress Anita Morris, who died before the film was finished.

Lucas kicked off 1990 by attending the opening of the third Star Tours attraction at the MGM Studios Theme Park in Florida, at which he announced that he planned to begin working on the second trilogy of *Star Wars* movies within the next five or six years. Of course, it would transpire that fans would have to wait rather longer than that to see the first of these movies. However, at least they had word from the horse's mouth that there would actually be a second trilogy, which did much to gladden the hearts of *Star Wars* fans everywhere.

In the meantime there were other projects to attend to, among them the television series *Maniac Mansion*, which had originated in a computer game created by the games division of Lucasfilm. First broadcast on the Family Channel in September 1990, it centred round the comic antics of the gadget-

138

obsessed Edison family (among them brother and sister Ike and Tina Edison) who just happen to have a comet in their basement.

Then, in March 1991, Lucas received the Irving G. Thalberg award at the Academy Awards ceremony, which recognized his immense achievements in the cinema, despite the fact that he was still no longer a member of the DGA nor the AMPAS. The highest honour the Academy could bestow, Lucas thus joined the likes of movie giants Alfred Hitchcock, Cecil B. de Mille and Walt Disney, all of whom had been former recipients.

At the time Lucas received his lifetime achievement award he was in the midst of his biggest television project. This was *The Young Indiana Jones Chronicles*, a lavish 22-part series, the seeds for which had been sown in the prologue of *Indiana Jones and the Last Crusade*, plus the idea for an educational CD-ROM titled *A Walk Through Early Twentieth-Century History with Indiana Jones*.

A massive undertaking, the shows - which were given feature production values - followed Indy's adventures as a child between 1908 and 1910 (in which he was played by Corey Carrier) and as a young man between 1916 and 1920 (during which he was played by Sean Patrick Flanery). Meanwhile, Broadway actor George Hall bookended the stories as the wizened 93-year-old Indy, who recalls his adventures from the present day. Given these timescales, Indy found himself involved in such historical incidents as the Battle of Verdun, during which 750, 000 men lost their lives in less than a week, and Ireland's Easter Rebellion. He also encountered such real life characters as Teddy Roosevelt, Pablo Picasso, Sigmund Freud, Leo Tolstoy, Thomas Edison, Pancho Villa and Winston Churchill, thus making the series an educational experience as well as an entertaining one.

Each episode of *The Young Indiana Jones Chronicles* cost in the region of $4m to make, and the series shot in over 20 countries, among them Africa, India, China, Britain, Spain, France, Turkey, Russia, Czechoslovakia, Italy, Austria and America. The shooting schedule ultimately lasted over three years and made use of state of the art effects technology in a bid to keep production costs down. The series, which luxuriated in such titles as *My First Adventure*, *The Trenches of Hell*, *The Phantom Train of Doom*, *Masks of Evil* and *Hollywood Follies*, also made use of top talent. Among the writers who contributed scripts to the show (all of which were based on stories by Lucas) were Frank Darabont *(The Shawshank Redemption)*, Jonathan Hensleigh *(Die Hard with a Vengeance)*, Rosemary Anne Sisson *(Upstairs, Downstairs)* Carrie Fisher *(Postcards from the Edge)* and Ben Burtt *(The Great Heep)*, whilst directors included Billé August (*Pelle the Conqueror*), Mike Newell (*Four Weddings and a Funeral*), Gavin Millar (*Dreamchild*), Joe Johnston (*The Rocketeer*), Simon Wincer (*Free Willy*), Nicolas Roeg (*Don't Look Now*), Peter MacDonald (*Rambo III*), Terry Jones (*Personal Services*), Dick Maas (*Amsterdamned*), stunt arranger Vic Armstrong and sound effects wiz Ben Burtt.

Among the starry cast of supporting players were such names as Margaret Tyzack, Lukas Haas, Max von Sydow, Michael Gough, Dorothy Tutin, Elizabeth Hurley, Vanessa Redgrave, Tom Bell, Ronald Fraser, Freddie Jones, Joss Ackland, Christopher Lee, Harry Enfield, Liz Smith, Kenneth Cranham, Tim McInnerny, Timothy Spall, Terry Jones, Catherine Zeta Jones, Peter Firth, Bob Peck, Tom Courtney, Cyril Cusack, Anna Massey, Jeroen Krabbé and Anne Heche, plus such familiar Lucasfilm players as William Hootkins, Paul Freeman, Ian McDiarmid, Anthony Daniels and Harrison Ford, the latter appearing in the episode titled *Mystery of the Blues*.

The series was produced by Rick McCallum and involved such technical personnel as cameraman David Tattersall and production designers Gavin Bocquet and Ricky Eyres, whilst Joel McNeely and Laurence Rosenthal provided the music, the latter also composing the catchy title theme. As always, Lucas executive produced, using the series as a grounds for experimentation in computer generated imagery, a process he hoped to make much use of in the long-awaited *Star Wars* prequels. This involved creating CGI sets and turning a crowd of fifteen extras into one of hundreds, all of which helped to keep costs down.

However, whilst the series proved a joy to work on for all concerned, it didn't fare too well in the all-important ratings. It premiered on the ABC network on 4 March 1992 and began strongly thanks to the advance publicity and the audience's love of the *Indy* feature films. Unfortunately, viewing figures began decline as the series progressed, with many complaining that it lacked the kind of action they had hoped for, whilst others criticized the plots for being on the dull side. Nevertheless, the series' strong production values earned it a hefty 26 Emmy nominations during its run, of which it went on to win 16. These were for the episodes titled *My First Adventure* (which won for art direction, costume design, editing and make-up), *Spring Break Adventure* (art direction, costume design, editing and make-up), *The Trenches of Hell* (sound editing), *Demons of Deception* (sound mixing), *Mystery of the Blues* (cinematography, sound mixing and music direction) and *The Scandal of 1920* (costume design, music composition, visual effects).

Despite his involvement in *The Young Indiana Jones Chronicles*, this wasn't the only project Lucas had on the go at the time. Several of the people who worked on the television series also found themselves involved in a movie called *Radioland Murders*, among them producer Rick McCallum, cinematographer David Tattersall, production designer Gavin Bocquet and composer Joel McNeeley. This was a story Lucas had been tinkering with for some 20 years, which he now finally assigned to Willard Huyck, Gloria Katz, Jeff Reno and Ron Osborn to script.

Billed as a 'romantic mystery-comedy', the story, set in 1939, follows the comic events one evening during the launch of a new Chicago-based radio network, WBN. A murderer is on the loose in the building, and a hapless writer (played by Brian Benben) finds himself accused of the crimes, so he tries to discover the identity of the killer himself, all the time trying to woo back his wife (played by Mary Stuart Masterson), who just happens to be the daughter of the network's bullish owner (Ned Beatty).

Directed by British comedian-turned-director Mel Smith (*The Tall Guy*), the $10m production was executive produced by Lucas and, like the *Young Indy* series, made much use of CGI sets and effects, again to test the hardware for the future *Star Wars* films. A breakneck farce in the manner of thirties and forties comedies, it was Lucas's love letter to the golden age of radio. Yet despite Lucas's name on the credits, plus a cast that included such familiar faces as George Burns, Brion James, Christopher Lloyd, Scott Campbell, Corbin Bernsen, Michael Lerner, Jeffrey Tambor, Rosemary Clooney, Billy Barty, Candy Clark, Bo Hopkins, Harvey Korman, Peter MacNicol and Bobcat Goldthwaite, the film failed to find an audience, perhaps because Woody Allen had already explored the same territory with his similarlyl themed *Radio Days*.

Said *Variety* of the movie, 'George Lucas collaborated previously with screenwriters Willard Huyck and Gloria Katz on *Howard the Duck*, and in terms of recalling that fiasco, *Radioland Murders* does pretty much everything but quack. A wild farce with more than one-hundred speaking parts, [it] offers scant appeal to the MTV generation and is too frenetic for anyone who might appreciate its Golden-Age-of-Radio setting... For the most part [it] feels like a theme park ride without an exit.'

Though he must have been disappointed with *Radioland Murders*' commercial and critical reception, Lucas was too busy to be distracted for long, for with the twentieth anniversary of *Star Wars* now approaching, he decided to revisit the central trilogy and, with the aid of the technology he'd been experimenting with on *Young Indy* and *Radioland*, decided to improve the three movies in several key areas.

Given the advances in technology as seen in such films as *Terminator 2: Judgement Day*, *Jurassic Park* and *Forrest Gump*, Lucas was now able to tinker with *Star Wars*, *Empire* and *Jedi* and present them as he'd originally intended. This digital technology would allow him to improve and preserve the sound and picture quality of the films, which had deteriorated somewhat over twenty years. These Special Editions, as they came to be known, would also act as a curtain raiser to the new trilogy of prequels, which Lucas had finally officially announced were on their way in May 1995, much to the jubilation of fans.

Whilst work was going on preparing the original trilogy for re-release, thus allowing a whole new generation to see the movies large and loud on the big screen for the first time, Lucas had the foresight to first release the movies on video one last time, with THX sound. Astonishingly, despite their familiarity from countless television screenings, an incredible twenty-two million copies of *Star Wars*, *Empire* and *Jedi* flew off the shelves.

The Special Edition was of course not the first time Lucas had tinkered with *Star Wars*. When the original theatrical version was first released, it was simply titled *Star Wars*. With the release of *Empire*, it became *Star Wars: Episode IV - A New Hope*. Meanwhile, some opening day prints of the original lacked one of the film's comic highlights: Chewbacca's roar at a little cleaner droid onboard the Death Star. Aunt Beru's dialogue was also completely dubbed in all but the original print.

The Special Edition of *Star Wars* had much more radical changes than these minor tweaks. The original master print, which had been stored in a subterranean vault in Kansas at a temperature of 50 degrees, had nevertheless degenerated, despite the precautions taken. It was scratched and dirty and had suffered a 15 percent loss of colour. This negative just didn't have the quality required to strike 2000 prints for showing across America (a huge number given the original opened at just 32 cinemas!). A group of technicians, led by film restoration consultant Bob Hart, thus spent three years arduously restoring the print frame by frame. The film was also given a newly mixed THX soundtrack, which allowed sound designer Ben Burtt to create a much more dynamic sound environment. Composer John Williams and music editor Ken Wannberg also adjusted the mix of the music.

As well as these improvements, Lucas also wanted to add new effects footage to *Star Wars*. Supervised by ILM's Dennis Muren, the most notable of these additional effects was Han Solo's encounter with Jabba the Hutt, which had been cut from the original. The advances in CGI now meant that a computerised version of the Jabba familiar from *Jedi* could be added to the existing footage featuring Harrison Ford interacting with actor Declan Mullholland, who ended up on the cutting room floor a second time! A lengthy task, it took computer animator Steve Williams four months to complete the sequence, which allowed audiences to see a mobile Jabba for the first time, complete with slithery sound effects and a vocal track care of Ben Burtt.

Other sequences added to the movie included new second unit footage shot in Arizona showing the Imperial Stormtroopers searching for R2-D2 and C-3PO on Tatooine. This included a new CGI Dewback, all of which made the scene busier. The sequence showing the entry of Luke, Ben, R2-D2 and C-3PO into Mos Eisley in Luke's landspeeder was also expanded. This now included more people, plus CGI Rontos - beasts of burden based on the CGI brontosauruses seen in *Jurassic Park* - which the Jawas have a hard time controling after they are startled by Luke's landspeeder. The live action segments for this sequence were filmed using ILM staff and their friends and families, who were dressed up as desert dwellers and spent a day in front of a blue screen. Digital mattes, designed by Paul Huston, also made Mos Eisley look more like the bustling spaceport it was supposed to be.

The Rebel's base on the moon of Yavin was also given a facelift, complete with transport carts. The final space battle and the Rebels' assault on the Death Star were souped up, too. Virtual CGI models of Tie Fighters and X-Wings were added, again making the sequence look much busier than the original. All told, 109 new shots, amounting to four-and-a-half minutes of screen time, were added to *Star Wars* at a cost of $10m, which had of course been the budget of the original movie. Meanwhile, a further $5m was spent adding 158 new shots to *The Empire Strikes Back* and 70 new shots to *Return of the Jedi*.

In *Empire*, the sequences in the Cloud City were given a brush up, making them look more expansive and less claustrophobic, thanks to the inclusion of a handful of new exterior shots which better showed the size of the place. There were a few extra shots of the Wampa added too, which Lucas himself directed in a reconstructed set of the beast's snow cavern. The matte lines round vehicles in the battle of Hoth were also digitally adjusted - in the originals one could actually see through parts of the aircraft as they circled the AT-ATs! Meanwhile, in *Jedi*, the opening number of Lapti Nek was replaced by a new song, *Jedi*

Rocks, which now featured CGI members of the Max Rebo Band plus some new chorus girls. The cringe-making closing Ewok song was also thankfully replaced and the finale considerably expanded to take in the celebrations on Tatooine, Endor and Bespin, giving the conclusion of the film a more epic, interplanetary feel. The Imperial City of Coruscant is also shown for the first time in this sequence, offering a taste of things to come in the first *Star Wars* prequel, in which the city is a significant location.

News that the Special Editions were on the way, plus the three new prequels, created something of a bidding war between companies keen to exploit the movies' merchandising possibilities. Since *Star Wars*, merchandising and tie-ins with soft drink companies and fast food restaurants had become a way of life in Hollywood, and in 1996 Lucasfilm made the biggest promotional alliance in entertainment history with Pepsico, who paid a staggering $2bn for the rights to exploit *Star Wars* and its characters for five years on their drinks cans and in the various restaurants the company owned, among them Pizza Hutt, Taco Bell and KFC.

In the run up to the release of the Special Editions, *Return of the Jedi* finally made it to radio in October 1996. Broadcast in six half-hour episodes on National Public Radio, the adaptation starred Josh Fardon as Luke, Ed Asner as Jabba the Hutt, John Lithgow as Yoda and Anthony Daniels as C-3PO. Naturally, the publicity hoopla surrounding the eventual release of the Special Editions the following year was enormous. In America, *Star Wars* was released on 31 January, followed by *Empire* on 21 February and *Jedi* on 13 March. *Star Wars* fever was back, and as big as ever. Indeed, *Star Wars - The Special Edition* made $35m in its opening weekend, making it the biggest ever January opening in history, crushing such newcomers as the volcano epic *Dante's Peak* in the process. The cast was wheeled out again to promote the films, and even the usually reticent Harrison Ford agreed to attend a few events and do some interviews, as did the equally publicity-shy Lucas.

The process of bringing the three films back to the big screen in their improved form was chronicled in a publicity-grabbing television special titled *Making Magic: A Behind-the-Scenes Look at the Making of the Star Wars Trilogy Special Editions*, which contained interviews with all the cast (except for Alec Guinness), plus several key technical personnel, including producer Rick McCallum who, following his chores on *Young Indy*, had been given the trilogy to oversee, along with the three new movies.

Harrison Ford does his duty for the cameras

Star Wars opened in Britain on 20 March 1997 in a special premier for the Prince of Wales' Trust Fund. Lucas introduced the film himself, which raised £180,000 for the charity. In the following months, *Empire* and *Jedi* followed, and it was as if *Star Wars* had never been away. Indeed, the Special Edition of *Star Wars* itself went on to earn $140m, making it the sixth highest earner of the year behind *Men in Black*, *The Lost World*, *Liar, Liar*, *Air Force One* and *Jerry Maguire*. Meanwhile, *Empire* went on to make $64m and *Jedi* $77m, making the trilogy the most successful re-release in cinema history, easily beating the previous record holder, Disney's 1961 cartoon feature *One-Hundred-and-One Dalmations*, which had taken $60m in 1991. Indeed, the extra revenue generated by the re-release of *Star Wars* returned it to the position of number one box office champ, beating back *E.T.* to second place. The victory was short-lived, though, for the following year James Cameron's *Titanic* quickly snatched the number one spot when it went on to make well in excess of $1bn.

Still, there was always the first *Star Wars* prequel to come, and who knew what that was capable of making...

22

Millennium Bound

Pre-production on the *Star Wars* prequels began in the autumn of 1996. Instead of Elstree, the films would this time be based at the Millennium Studios in Leavesden, Hertfordshire. Formerly a Rolls-Royce factory, the studios had been created from scratch for the return of James Bond in *Goldeneye*.

Naturally, Lucas was tight-lipped about the exact content of the prequels. The title of the first of them, *Star Wars: Episode 1 - The Phantom Menace*, was revealed to the world on 25 September 1998, after such working titles as *Balance of the Force*, *Rise of the Empire*, *Genesis*, *Children of the Force*, *The Clone Wars*, *The Beginning*, *Jedi Squad*, *Way of the Jedi*, *Crusaders of the Force*, *Guardians of the Force*, *Knights of the Force* and *Fall of the Jedi* had been considered. It was even rumoured that the chosen title of *The Phantom Menace* could change at the last moment, presumably in a bid to prevent pirate merchandising.

Despite Lucas's precautions, tantalising information about *The Phantom Menace* gradually began to seep out. Rumour had it that the story would take place some 32 years before the original *Star Wars* and would chart the rise and fall of Luke and Leia's father, Anakin Skywalker, explaining how the greatest Jedi Knight in the galaxy came to be seduced by the dark side of The Force to become the evil Darth Vader. Given this scenario, *The Phantom Menace* would feature mostly new characters, with only the younger versions of Anakin/Vader, Obi-Wan Kenobi, Yoda, R2-D2 and C-3PO playing significant roles in both trilogies. It was also revealed that the film would be set in three principal locations: the city of Coruscant - home of the Galactic Senate, the Imperial Palace and the Jedi Temple (Coruscant had been seen briefly at the end of the Special Edition of *Return of the Jedi*); Tatooine; and the swamp planet of Naboo.

Besides writing and executive producing the *Star Wars* prequels, Lucas announced that he would be directing at least the first one himself, making this his first full return to directing since *Star Wars*. Lucas had spent almost three years developing the script for *The Phantom Menace*, from 1995 to 1997, after which both Frank Darabont and Carrie Fisher are said to have given the dialogue a final polish. As he had done with that first epic *Star Wars* script in the seventies, Lucas beavered away at the new screenplay at the Skywalker Ranch from 9:30am through to 6:30pm most days, eschewing a computer for pencils and yellow legal tablets. And just as the original *Star Wars/Empire/Jedi* scripts were based on Lucas's epic original story, so too was *The Phantom Menace*, concentrating on its earliest narrative developments.

As Lucas was scribbling away, storyboard artists were already beginning to visualize his new concepts, developing the look of the vehicles, vessels and creatures required. Chief among these artists was visual concept designer Doug Chiang, who effectively filled the role of Ralph McQuarrie on the original trilogy. A former art director for ILM, Chiang had worked on such movies as *Terminator 2: Judgement Day*, *Jumanji* and *Forrest Gump*, so he was ideal for the job. By the end of 1996, Chiang and his team had produced over 1200 pieces of artwork for the movie.

The film's production re-united many Lucasfilm employees, among them producer Rick McCallum, who'd worked on *Young Indy* and the *Star Wars* Special Editions; cinematographer David Tattersall, who'd photographed several episodes of *Young Indy*, plus *Radioland Murders* (since when he'd also photographed such movies as *The Wind in the Willows* and *Con Air*); creature effects supervisor Nick Dudman, who had started his career as a make-up trainee with Stuart Freeborn on *The Empire Strikes Back*, after which he went on to work on *Return of the Jedi*, *Willow* and *Indiana Jones and the Last Crusade* (plus the likes of *Legend*, *Batman*, *Interview with the Vampire*, *Judge Dredd* and *The Fifth Element*); editor Paul Martin Smith who'd cut *Young*

Indy; stunt co-ordinator Nick Gillard, who'd worked on *Indiana Jones and the Temple of Doom*, *Indiana Jones and the Last Crusade* and *Young Indy*; costume designer Trisha Biggar, who'd worked on *Young Indy*; production designer Gavin Bocquet, who'd designed the sets for *Young Indy* and *Radioland Murders*; and composer John Williams.

In 1996, production designer Gavin Bocquet began to devote all his energies to *The Phantom Menace*, scouting for locations in Morocco, Portugal and Australia. Given that much of the film would centre on Tatooine and the town of Mos Espa, Bocquet also returned to Tunisia. Unfortunately, no records from the original *Star Wars* shoot survived, so Bocquet took *Star Wars* devotee David West Reynolds with him to track down the sites of Obi-Wan Kenobi's home and the entrance to Mos Eisley. Meanwhile, Trisha Biggar was given six months prior to shooting to design the film's hundreds of costumes, working on concepts with Doug Chiang and Lucas himself.

As soon as news broke that the *Star Wars* prequels were on their way, speculation began as to who would star in the first film. Early rumours had Mark Hamill returning to the fold to play Anakin Skywalker, Luke and Leia's father (which would have been interesting), while Shakespearian-actor-turned-movie-star Kenneth Brannagh was widely touted to take up the role of the young Obi-Wan Kenobi. Neither rumour came to pass, though Mark Hamill's son Nathan did find himself cast as an extra in the film.

Among other casting rumours circulating was that Charlton Heston would be voicing the younger Yoda, whilst Harry Connick Jr, David Warner and Michael Jackson would all somehow be involved. One story had it that the whole *Phantom Menace* cast would be entirely CGI, with the features of a young Alec Guinness superimposed on another actor! Even Anthony Daniels got in on the act, deliberately starting a false rumour that Macauley Culkin would be playing Anakin, just to see who would take the joke seriously (and quite a few people did). There were also rumours about which studio would actually distribute *The Phantom Menace*, given that the original *Star Wars* deal was no longer valid. Of course, Lucas still had strong links with Fox following the highly successful release of the Special Editions. Nevertheless, he also had a good relationship with Paramount via the *Indiana Jones* trilogy, plus MGM from *Willow* and Universal from *American Graffiti* and *Radioland Murders*. In fact it wouldn't be until 1998 that Fox's successful bid to release the movies was announced.

Preliminary casting actually began on *The Phantom Menace* in 1995, when

Liam Neeson and Ewan McGregor, mentor and student in *The Phantom Menace*

Lucas launched a worldwide search for an eight-year-old boy to play the very young Anakin Skywalker, and a thirteen-year-old girl to play Queen Amidala. Casting in earnest didn't begin until 1996, when casting director Robin Gurland began to interview prospective candidates for roles. This process lasted a full year, after which news began to filter through in May 1997.

Among the confirmations were that *Trainspotting* star Ewan MacGregor (also familiar from the likes of *Shallow Grave*, *The Pillow Book*, *Emma*, *Brassed Off*, *A Life Less Ordinary* and *Velvet Goldmine*) would be playing the younger Obi-Wan Kenobi, having beaten off such alleged competition as Brad Pitt, Leonardo DiCaprio and Russell Crowe for the part. An actor since the age of sixteen, McGregor (born in 1971) had been inspired to take up the profession by his film star uncle, Denis Lawson, who of course played Rebel pilot Wedge Antilles in the central trilogy.

Natalie Portman, Princess Amidala in The Phantom Menace

As the young Anakin Skywalker/Darth Vader, Colorado-born Jake Lloyd was chosen from over 6000 boys, among them other up-coming child actors like Eric Lloyd (*The Santa Clause*) and Nick Stahl (*The Man Without a Face*). Already a veteran of 34 commercials, such movies as *Unhook the Stars*, *Jingle All the Way* (with Arnold Schwarzenegger), and an episode of television's highly rated *E.R.*, nine-year-old Lloyd would be carrying the brunt of the new film's storyline. Meanwhile, as Queen Amidala, destined to become Anakin Skywalker's wife (therefore Luke and Leia's mother), sixteen-year-old Natalie Portman was cast. Already familiar from the likes of the acclaimed *Leon* (aka *The Professional*), *Heat*, *Beautiful Girls* and *Mars Attacks*, her role as Amidala was pivotal in *The Phantom Menace*, for which she apparently beat off the likes of Kate Winslet and Winona Ryder.

Elsewhere, Irish-born Liam Neeson, star of *Darkman*, *Schindler's List*, *Rob Roy* and *Michael Collins*, was set to play the role of Jedi Knight Qui-Gon Jinn, mentor to Anakin Skywalker and Obi-Wan Kenobi. One of the film's leading characters, Neeson pipped the likes of Morgan Freeman for the part. Born in Ballymena in 1952, Neeson originally studied to be a teacher before turning his hand to acting, which he subsequently studied at the Lyric Players' Theatre. Following a stint at Dublin's celebrated Abbey Theatre (at which Orson Welles had performed in his early years), Neeson finally made the jump to movies in 1980 with *Excalibur* in which he played Gawain, which he followed with the likes of *The Bounty*, *Krull* and *The Dead Pool*. An international star by the time he was cast in *The Phantom Menace*, he brought a certain gravitas to the cast, as had Alec Guinness and Peter Cushing before him.

Elsewhere, the film's supporting players included such original trilogy alumni as Anthony Daniels, back as C-3PO, Kenny Baker as R2-D2, Frank Oz as the voice and puppeteer of Yoda, and Ian McDiarmid as the scheming Senator (later Emperor) Palpatine, whose rise to power we now follow. Also appearing would be *Return of the Jedi*'s Warwick Davis as Wald, Anakin Skywalker's best friend. Since his work on Willow, Davis had appeared in the *Leprechaun* horror films and television's *Gulliver's Travels*. He'd also set up his own talent agency, Willow Personal Management, with his father-in-law Peter Borroughs, the purpose of which was to represent similarly diminutive actors and actresses.

Newcomers to the saga included Terence Stamp (*Billy Budd*, *The Adventures of Priscilla, Queen of the Desert*) as Supreme Chancellor Valorum; Hugh Quarshie (*Highlander*, *Nightbreed*) as Captain Panaka; Brian Blessed (*Flash Gordon*, *Robin Hood: Prince of Thieves*) as the CGI character Boz Nass, king of the swamp planet Naboo; Celia Imrie (television's *Pat and Margaret*) as fighter pilot Bravo Five; Adrian Dunbar (*Hear My Song*, *The Crying Game*) as Bail Organa, future foster-father of Princess Leia; Pernilla August (*Young Indy*, *Best Intentions*) as Shmi Skywalker, Anakin's mother and Luke and Leia's grandmother; Samuel L. Jackson (*Pulp Fiction*, *Jurassic Park*) as the previously much-mentioned Mace Windu; Ahmed Best as the comical CGI character Jar Jar Binks; and newcomer Ray Park, an international martial arts champion and stunt double (*Mortal Kombat: Annihilation)*, as the villainous Darth Maul.

The original budget for *The Phantom Menace* was first estimated at an extremely conservative $40m, though ultimately it would clock in at $115m, owing to the cost of the film's ground-breaking effects (though it was still a snip when compared to Titanic's $200m price tag). Given the nature of these effects, plus the new storylines, secrecy was paramount on *The Phantom Menace*. So much so that every member of the cast and crew had to sign a non-disclosure clause in their contract, banning them from discussing the film's plot. Meanwhile, all locations were surrounded by a patrolled barbed wire fence, with access available only via a main checkpoint with a photo ID swipe card (even George Lucas had one), making some wonder whether they were working on a movie or about to make a military strike. Clearly, the making of *The Phantom Menace* was a major event in cinema history. Lucas must have thought so too, for a documentary camera team, headed by director Jon Shenk, followed Lucas and the making of the movie from day one.

Principal photography on *The Phantom Menace* took 65 days to complete, though Lucas did return to Leavesden in August 1998 for pick-up shots. The heat was then on to complete the effects shots (almost 2000 of them, at a cost of $60m) and post production chores in time to meet the US release date of 21 May 1999, which was later brought forward to 19 May (a Wednesday), supposedly to allow diehard fans a chance to see the film first before the weekend rush of family audiences. Among the effects shots occupying most of ILM's time was the film's climactic battle scene, which involved 3000 CGI alien infantrymen fighting 4000 battle droids in one of the movie's most visually spectacular scenes.

British audiences would have to wait until 16 July 1999 to see the movie, though 120,000 hardcore fans from the UK and Europe actually made the trip to the States to see the film at the earlier date. For those who could afford to attend, but didn't want to fly to America, there was also the London premiere on 14 July in aid of The Cinema and Television Benevolent Fund. Attended by

Jake Lloyd - the shapes of things to come

The Prince of Wales, the movie was the official 1999 Royal Film Performance. Meanwhile, other release dates announced included Finland (6 August), Iceland (13 August) and Denmark (20 August), while Greece, Belgium and France would have to wait until October to see the film, owing to the lengthy dubbing process.

As post production progressed, Ballantine author Terry Brooks busied himself adapting Lucas's screenplay for the inevitable novelization (which quickly shot into the best seller charts when published), whilst toy manufacturers Kenner started to produce their line of spin-off figures and vehicles. By November 1998, Lucas had released the first teaser poster for the film, which simply featured Jake Lloyd as the young Anakin Skywalker walking across the sands of Tatooine. Closer inspection revealed that the boy's shadow was in the shape of his older alter ego, Darth Vader. November 17 also saw the release of the first theatrical trailer for *The Phantom Menace*. Though just over two minutes in length, audiences were actually paying to see this preview, which was playing

154

at a selected 75 US screens, after which many of them left before the main feature began. Needless to say, the trailer was greeted with rapturous applause, just as it was when it played in the UK for the first time on 16 December 1998.

In November 1998, John Williams began working on the score for *The Phantom Menace*, which took about ten weeks to complete. He then recorded the music at his regular haunt, Abbey Road Studios, in February 1999 using The London Symphony Orchestra (some members of which had played in the original *Star Wars* sessions). At the time of recording, the running time of the movie was approximately two hours and fifteen minutes, for which the composer provided in excess of 75 minutes of music. Williams' soundtrack was then released by Sony Classical on 4 May, and though it kicked off with his celebrated *Star Wars* theme, it featured entirely new themes and motifs, save for the occasional sly reference to the previous scores, most notably in the cue titled Anakin's Theme, which contained a subtle reference to Darth Vader's Theme, as a portent of things to come for the young Anakin.

One of Williams' most spectacular scores, it was greeted with great enthusiasm and quickly soared to the top of the soundtrack chart. However, some fans who bought the album prior to the film's release were a little annoyed when they read through the album's track list, for the cue titles, such as *Qui-Gon's Noble End* and *Qui-Gon's Funeral*, gave away the film's ending. Some reviewers actually warned readers of this.

By this time the official one-sheet poster for *The Phantom Menace* was widely displayed in America. Painted by Drew Struzan and accompanied by the tag line, 'Every saga has a beginning', it was very much in the style of Struzan's eye-catching posters for the Special Editions and featured the young Anakin Skywalker surrounded by the likes of Qui-Gon Jinn, Queen Amidala, the young Obi-Wan Kenobi, Jar Jar Binks, R2-D2 and C-3PO, whilst in the background the evil Darth Maul scowls over the scene.

By now interest in the movie was reaching fever pitch. Just as queues started forming days before the openings of *Star Wars*, *Empire* and *Jedi*, so they did for *The Phantom Menace*. In fact, an incredible 42 days before the film opened, a hardcore group of fifty fans began to queue outside Mann's Chinese Theatre in Hollywood. This proved to be something of a media event in itself, given that the group (formed by Tim Doyle, Philip Nokov and Lincoln Gasking) broadcast their activities worldwide on the internet and were themselves the subject of many television and print interviews and features as a consequence. However, while the group's website (www.countingdown.com) was definitely pro-*Star Wars*, there was a growing backlash to the sheer scale of the hype surrounding *The Phantom Menace* (mostly media-fuelled), hence the advent of such sites as http://www.ihatestarwars.com, through which dissenters voiced their hatred of the series.

For Lucas, though, the internet proved to be one of his most important marketing tools. Just as Gary Kurtz had toured the sci-fi conventions to help drum up interest in the original *Star Wars* back in 1977, Lucas was now able to tap straight into the homes of fans via the internet, through which those online could watch the trailer at their own convenience and read up on the latest facts and gossip on the movie. Indeed, when the trailer was first put out on the internet, the site had more than a million hits in its first week!

Finally, the long wait was over, and at one minute past midnight on 19 May 1999, *Star Wars: Episode 1 - The Phantom Menace* was released. Given the enormous amount of hype, it was inevitable that the film would open big. Indeed, it quickly beat the opening day record of $26m set by *The Lost World: Jurassic Park* in 1997 and went on to rake in an incredible $28.542m, of which it had made $7.5m by six am thanks to the through-the-night screenings! And this despite some pretty mixed reviews. But mixed reviews were nothing new for Lucas. The original *Star Wars* had been given a mixed reception by the critics in 1977, yet this didn't prevent it from going on to become a monster hit. With *The Phantom Menace*, it looked like history was about to repeat itself.

'Lucas's childlike vision is beginning to look merely childish', commented *Newsweek*, going on to ask, 'Is the hunger for *Star Wars* so insatiable that the audience won't notice that this epochal event is actually a little... dull?'. *Rolling Stone* was equally unenthusiastic, commenting, 'The actors are wallpaper, the jokes are juvenile, there's no romance and the dialogue lands with the thud of a computer instruction manual.' Even the usually upbeat *Variety* had its reservations: 'As the most widely anticipated and heavily-hyped film of modern times, *Star Wars: Episode 1 - The Phantom Menace* can scarcely help being a let-down on some levels, but it's too bad that it disappoints on so many. It is neither captivating nor transporting, for it lacks any emotional pull, as well as the sense of wonder and awe that marks the best works of sci-fi/fantasy.'

More upbeat was *The New York Times*, which wrote, 'It sustains the gee-whiz spirit of the series and offers a swashbuckling extragalactic getaway, creating illusions that are even more plausible than the kitchen-raiding raptors of *Jurassic Park*', to which *The Calgary Sun* added, '*The Phantom Menace* proves that Lucas still knows how to capture the imagination of young and old.'

However, as one pundit pointed out, despite the mostly negative press reaction, the film was practically critic proof. Some fans were indeed disappointed with the film overall, commenting that the characters were two-dimensional, that the effects overwhelmed the story (contrary to the promises of Lucas and producer Rick McCallum) and that some of the characters, such as the would-be comical Jar Jar Binks, were actually a little annoying. All were impressed by the early speeder race, however, and Darth Maul and his amazing double-bladed lightsaber went down a storm, especially with younger viewers who were drawn by the character's eye-catching red and black make-up.

Despite Lucas's attempts to safeguard the film from piracy, a week after the US opening, copies of it were already appearing in shops in Hong Kong and Macau. Widely available, video CDs of *The Phantom Menace* were selling for around HK$30.

Before *The Phantom Menace* was even completed, rumours about the next two prequels began to form. During the 1998 re-shoots, it was claimed that Lucas had shot some footage of Mos Eisley for Episode Two. It was also later confirmed that Lucas had actually bought a fifteen-square-mile area of Tunisian desert for a reported $100,000, confirming that the saga had not yet finished with Tatooine. Then came the announcement that Episodes Two and Three would be shot in Australia at Fox's new studios in Sydney. Directors bandied about to helm these episodes included Steven Spielberg, Frank Darabont, David Fincher and Luc Besson, though Lucas didn't rule out that he might helm them himself. There was also talk that the two films would be shot back to back, as had been the case with *Back to the Future II* and *III* in the late eighties.

Meanwhile, all talk of the three sequels to *Star Wars* (bringing the grand total to nine films) seemed to have been abandoned, given the timescales involved to get them all made, though in a 1997 interview Lucas admitted that it might be fun to make three more films centred round the adventures of the older Han, Luke and Leia, an idea he had mentioned in passing to Mark Hamill. Though whether Lucas would be able to persuade Hamill, Carrie Fisher and Harrison Ford to revive their characters is another matter entirely. As it was, Lucas was having trouble trying to get Ford to commit to a fourth *Indiana Jones* adventure which, like the *Star Wars* prequels, had also been long-touted. Again, rumour went into overdrive regarding the new Indy film, said to be titled *Indiana Jones and the Lost City of Atlantis* and based on a script by Jeffrey Boam (other titles said to have been considered include *Indiana Jones and the Fountain of Youth*).

One thing is certain, however. The phenomenal success of *The Phantom Menace* will firmly place Lucas in the cinematic history books as one of the most admired, innovative and commercially successful filmmakers of all time - a man with a passion for movies and moviemaking, so much so that he is prepared to re-invest vast amounts of his personal profit back into the industry so as to safeguard its future, and to help develop the technology required to tell the kind of stories he is interested in making.

Some have described *The Phantom Menace* as the most anticipated film of the century, all of which must have piled the pressure on Lucas (and ILM) to deliver the goods. Indeed, predictions of a $1bn box office take were bandied around even before the film had opened. Consequently, other studios wisely put the release of their own would-be summer blockbusters on hold for a reported seven weeks, there being little point in putting them out in competition against the all-consuming *Phantom Menace*.

It barely seems to matter whether *The Phantom Menace* is any good or not. Its high profile has guaranteed that it will more than cover its costs. Indeed, such over-hyped films as *Batman* and *Titanic* pale besides the pre-release frenzy surrounding the film. In truth, it's hard to think of another film that, six months prior to being released, had prospective audiences talking about its characters like old friends, even though the likes of Queen Amidala, Jar Jar Binks and Qui-Gon Jinn were completely new to the series. Such was the draw of the *Star Wars* films and the power of Lucas's creative and marketing prowess.

Despite all the pressures and expectations, Lucas has always done things his way. It's been his vision every step down the line. Often this has worked; only occasionally has he put a foot wrong commercially or artistically. Yet even miscalculations like *Howard the Duck* have proved to be learning experiences, providing valuable lessons. And if these have been learned, then the world won't be George Lucas's oyster - the universe will be.

Appendix One

USC Films, Shorts and Documentaries made by George Lucas

Look at Life

Made 1965

Animation: George Lucas

Herbie

Made : 1966

Director : George Lucas, Paul Golding

1.42.08

Made : 1966

Screenplay : George Lucas

Director: George Lucas

The Emperor

Made : 1967

Director : George Lucas

THX 1138: 4EB (Electronic Labyrinth)

Made : 1967

Screenplay : George Lucas

Director : George Lucas

Editor: George Lucas

Anyone Loved in a Pretty Town

Made : 1967

Screenplay : George Lucas, Paul Golding

Director : George Lucas

6:18:67 (McKenna's Gold Documentary)

Made : 1967

Director : George Lucas

Filmmaker (Francis Ford Coppola Documentary)

Made : 1968

Screenplay: George Lucas

Director : George Lucas

Photography: George Lucas

Editor : George Lucas

Appendix Two

Chronological filmography of features involving George Lucas as either writer, director or executive producer.

THX: 1138

Year of Release: 1971

Running Time: 88m

Production Company: American Zoetrope

Releasing Company: Warner Bros..

Executive Producer: Francis Ford Coppola

Producer: Lawrence Sturhahn

Screenplay: George Lucas, Walter Murch

Story: George Lucas

Director: George Lucas

Photography: Dave Meyers, Albert Kihn

Music: Lalo Schifrin

Editor: George Lucas

Production Design: Michael Haller

Costumes: Donald Longhurst

Sound: Walter Murch, Louis Yates, Jim Manson

Titles Design: Hal Barwood

Cast: Robert Duvall (THX 1138), Donald Pleasence (SEN 5241), Maggie McOmie (LUH 3417), Don Pedro Colley (SRT), Ian Wolfe (PTO), Sid Haig (NCH), Gary Alan Marsh (CAM), Eugene I. Stillman (JOT), Johnny Weissmuller, Jr (Robot)

American Graffiti

Year of Release: 1973

Running Time: 110m

Production Company: Lucasfilm/Coppola Company

Releasing Company: Universal

Producer: Francis Ford Coppola, Gary Kurtz

Screenplay: George Lucas, Gloria Katz, Willard Huyck

Director: George Lucas

Photography: Ron Eveslage, Jan D'Alquen

Music: Bill Haley and the Comets, Buddy Holly, The Big Bopper, The Platters, Chuck Berry, Fats Domino, The Beach Boys, and others

Editor: Verna Fields, Marcia Lucas

Production Design: Dennis Clark

Costumes: Aggue Guerard Rodgers

Sound: Walter Murch

Visual Consultant: Haskell Wexler

Cast: Richard Dreyfus (Curt Henderson), Ron Howard (Steve Bolander), Candy Clark (Debbie), Charles Martin Smith (Terry "The Toad" Fields), Paul LeMat (John Milner), Cindy Williams (Laurie), Mackenzie Phillips (Carol), Disc Joockey (Wolfman Jack [aka Robert Smith]), Harrison Ford (Bob Falfa), Bo Hopkins (Joe), Manuel Padilla, Jr (Carlos), Beau Gentry (Ants), Jim Bohan (Holstein), Kathleen Quinlan (Peg)

Star Wars (aka Star Wars: Episode IV - A New Hope)

Year of Release: 1977

Running Time: 121m

Production Company: Lucasfilm

Releasing Company: Twentieth Century Fox

Producer: Gary Kurtz

Screenplay: George Lucas

Director: George Lucas

Photography: Gilbert Taylor

Music: John Williams

Editor: Paul Hirsch, Marcia Lucas, Richard Chew

Production Design: John Barry

Costumes: John Mollo

Special Effects: John Dykstra

Sound: Ben Burtt

2nd Unit Photography: Carroll Ballard, Rick Clemente, Robert Dalva, Tak Fujimoto, Bruce Logan

Concept Design: Ralph McQuarrie

Make-up and Creature Effects: Stuart Freeborn, Rick Baker

Cast: Mark Hamill (Luke Skywalker), Carrie Fisher (Princess Leia Organa), Harrison Ford (Han Solo), Peter Cushing (Grand Moff Tarkin), Alec Guinness (Obi-Wan Kenobi), Anthony Daniels (C-3PO), Kenny Baker (R2-D2), Peter Mayhew (Chewbacca), Dave Prowse (Darth Vader), James Earl Jones (Voice of Darth Vader), Phil Brown (Uncle Owen Lars), Shelagh Fraser (Aunt Beru Lars), Alex McGrindle (General Dodonna), Eddie Byrne (General Willard), Drewe Henley (Red Leader), Denis Lawson (Wedge Antilles), William Hootkins (Red Six - Porkins), Biggs Darklighter (Garrick Hagon), Jeremy Sinden (Gold Two), Don Henderson (General Taggi), Richard Le Parmentier (General Motti), Jack Purvis (Jawa)

More American Graffiti

Year of Release: 1979

Running Time: 111m

Production Company: Lucasfilm

Releasing Company: Twentieth Century Fox

Executive Producer: George Lucas

Producer: Howard Kazanjian

Screenplay: B.W.L. Norton

Director: B.W.L. Norton

Photography: Caleb Deschanel

Music: Various

Editor: Tina Hirsch

Production Design: Ray Storey

Costumes: Aggie Guerrard Rodgers

Cast: Ron Howard (Steve Bolander), Candy Clark (Debbie), Cindy Williams (Laurie Bolander), Charles Martin Smith (Terry "The Toad" Fields), Paul LeMat (John Milner), Mackenzie Phillips (Carol), Bo Hopkins (Joe)

The Empire Strikes Back (aka Star Wars: Episode V - The Empire Strikes Back)

Year of Release: 1980

Running Time: 124m

Production Company: Lucasfilm

Releasing Company: Twentieth Century Fox

Executive Producer: George Lucas

Producer: Gary Kurtz

Screenplay: Leigh Brackett, Lawrence Kadan

Story: George Lucas

Director: Irvin Kershner

Photography: Peter Suschitzsky

Music: John Williams

Editor: Paul Hirsch

Production Design: Norman Reynolds

Costumes: John Mollo

Special Effects: Brian Johnson, Richard Edlund, Dennis Muren, Bruce Nicholson

Sound: Bill Varney, Steve Maslow, Gregg Landaker, Peter Sutton, Ben Burtt, Randy Thom

2nd Unit Director: John Barry, Gary Kurtz (uncredited), Peter MacDonald, Harley Cockliss

2nd Unit Photography: Chris Menges, Geoff Glover

Concept Design: Ralph McQuarrie

Make-up and Creature Effects: Stuart Freeborn

Cast: Mark Hamill (Luke Skywalker), Harrison Ford (Han Solo), Carrie Fisher (Princess Leia Organa), Billy Dee Williams (Lando Calrissian), Anthony Daniels (C-3PO), R2-D2 (Kenny Baker), Dave Prowse (Darth Vader), James Earl Jones (Voice of Darth Vader), Peter Mayhew (Chewbacca), Alec Guinness (Obi-Wan Kenobi), Yoda (Frank Oz), Jeremy Bulloch (Boba Fett), Jack Purvis (Chief Ugnaught), Clive Revill (Voice of Emperor), Kenneth Colley (Admiral Piett), Julian Glover (Captain Veers), Denis Lawson (Wedge Antilles)

Kagemusha (aka The Shadow Warrior/The Double)

Year of Release: 1980

Running Time: 179m

Production Company: Toho

Releasing Company: Twentieth Century Fox

Executive Producer: George Lucas, Francis Ford Coppola (international version)

Producer: Akira Kurosawa, Tomoyuki Tanaka

Screenplay: Akira Kurosawa, Masato Ide

Director: Akira Kurosawa

Photography: Takao Saito, Asaichi Nakai, Kazuo Miyagawa, Shoji Ueda

Music: Shinichiro Ikebe

Production Design: Yoshiro Muraki

Tatsuya Nakadai (Kagemusha/Shingen Takeda), Tsutomu Yamazaki (Nobukado Takeda), Kota Yui (Takemaru), Kenichi Hagiwara (Katsuyori Takeda), Hideo Murata (Baba), Daisuke Ryu (Oda), Shuji Otaki (Yamagata)

CHRONOLOGICAL FILMOGRAPHY

Raiders of the Lost Ark

Year of Release: 1981

Running Time: 115m

Production Company: Lucasfilm

Releasing Company: Paramount

Executive Producer: George Lucas, Howard Kazanjian

Producer: Frank Marshall

Screenplay: Lawrence Kasdan

Story: George Lucas, Philip Kaufman

Director: Steven Spielberg

Photography: Douglas Slocombe

Music: John Williams

Editor: Michael Kahn

Production Design: Norman Reynolds

Costumes: Deborah Nadoolman

Special Effects: Richard Edlund, Kit West, Bruce Nicholson, Joe Johnston

Sound: Bill Varney, Steve Maslow, Gregg Landaker, Roy Charman, Ben Burt

2nd Unit Director: Michael Moore

2nd Unit Photography: Paul Beeson

Stunt Co-ordinator: Glenn Randall, Peter Diamond

Cast: Harrison Ford (Indiana Jones), Karen Allen (Marion Ravenwood), Paul Freeman (Belloq), Ronald Lacey (Toht), Denholm Elliott (Marcus Brody), John Rhys-Davies (Sallah), Wolf Kahler (Dietrich), Anthony Higgins (Gobler), Alfred Molina (Satipo), Vic Tablian (Barranca), Pat Roach (Tough German), Frank Marshall (Pilot)

Body Heat

Year of Release: 1981

Running Time: 113m

Production Company: The Ladd Company

Releasing Company: Warner Bros..

Exectuive Producer: George Lucas (uncredited)

Producer: Fred T. Gallo

Screenplay: Lawrence Kasdan

Director: Lawrence Kasdan

Photography: Richard H. Kline

Music: John Barry

Editor: Carol Littleton

Production Design: Bill Kenney

Costumes: Renie Conley

Cast: William Hurt (Ned Racine), Kathleen Turner (Matty Walker), Ted Danson (Peter Lowenstein), Richard Crenna (Edmund Walker), J.A. Preston (Oscar Grace), Mickey Rourke (Teddy Lewis), Kim Zimmer (Mary Ann), Jane Halleren (Stella), Lanna Saunders (Roz Kraft)

Twice Upon a Time

Year of Release: 1982

Running Time: 75m

Production Company: Lucasfilm/Korty Films/The Ladd Company

Releasing Company: Warner Bros..

Executive Producer: George Lucas

Producer: John Korty, Bill Couturie, Charles Swenson

Screenplay: John Korty, Charles Swenson, Suella Kennedy, Bill Couturie

Story: John Korty, Bill Couturie, Suella Kennedy

Director: John Korty, Charles Swenson

Editor: Jennifer Gallagher

Music: Dawn Atkinson, Ken Melville

Sound: Walt Kraemer

Voices: Hamilton Kamp, Paul Frees, Marshall Efron, Julia Payne, James Cranna, Judith Kahan Kampmann, Lorenzo Music

Return of the Jedi (aka Star Wars: Episode VI - Return of the Jedi)

Year of Release: 1983

Running Time: 133m

Production Company: Lucasfilm

Releasing Company: Twentieth Century Fox

Executive Producer: George Lucas

Producer: Howard Kazanjian

Screenplay: Lawrence Kasdan, George Lucas

Story: George Lucas

Director: Richard Marquand

Photography: Alan Hume

Music: John Williams

Editor: Marcia Lucas, Sean Barton, Duwayne Dunham

Production Design: Norman Reynolds

Costumes: Aggie Guerard Rodgers, Nilo Rodis-Jamero

Special Effects: Richard Edlund, Ken Ralston, Dennis Muren, Phil Tippettt

Sound: Ben Burtt

Make-up and Creature Effects: Stuart Freeborn, Phil Tippettt

Concept Design: Ralph McQuarrie

Cast: Mark Hamill (Luke Skywalker), Harrison Ford (Han Solo), Carrie Fisher (Princess Leia Organa), Billy Dee Williams (Lando Calrissian), Anthony Daniels (C-3PO), Kenny Baker (R2-D2), Dave Prowse (Darth Vader), James Earl Jones (Voice of Darth Vader), Sebastian Shaw (Anakin Skywalker), Ian McDiarmid (Emperor Palpatine), Frank Oz (Yoda), Alex Guinness (Obi-Wan Kenobi), Michael Pennington (Moff Jerjerrod), Kenneth Colley (Bib Fortuna), Denis Lawson (Wedge Antilles), Tim Rose (Admiral Ackbar), Warwick Davis (Wicket), Jeremy Bulloch (Boba Fett), Femi Taylor (Oola), Claire Davenport (Gargan), Robert Watts (AT-ST Driver), Richard Marquand (AT-ST Driver)

Indiana Jones and the Temple of Doom

Year of Release: 1984

Running Time: 118m

Production Company: Lucasfilm

Releasing Company: Paramount

Executive Producer: George Lucas, Frank Marshall

Producer: Robert Watts

Screenplay: Willard Huyck, Gloria Katz

Story: George Lucas

Director: Steven Spielberg

Photography: Douglas Slocombe

Music: John Williams

Editor: Michael Kahn

Production Design: Elliot Scott

Costumes: Anthony Powell

Special Effects: Dennis Muren, Michael McAlister, Lorne Peterson, George Gibbs

Sound: Ben Burtt, Simon Kaye, Gary Summers, Randy Thom, Ben Burtt

2nd Unit Director: Michael Moore, Frank Marshall, Glenn Randall, Kevin Donnelly

2nd Unit Photography: Allen Daviau, Jack Cooperman

Additonal Photography: Paul Beeson

Stunt Co-oedinator: Vic Armstrong, Glenn Randall

Choreography: Danny Daniels

Cast: Harrison Ford (Indiana Jones), Kate Capshaw (Willie Scott), Ke Huy Quan (Short Round), Roshan Seth (Chattar Lal), Amrish Puri (Mola Ram), Philip Stone (Captain Blumenthal), David Yip (Wu Han), Dan Aykroyd (Airport Rep), Roy Chiao (Lao Che), Ric Young (Kao Kan), Chua Kan Joo (Chen), Pat Roach (Guard)

Mishima

Year of Release: 1985

Running Time: 120m

Production Company: Lucasfilm/American Zoetrope/Filmlink

Releasing Company: Warner Bros..

Executive Producer: George Lucas, Francis Ford Coppola

Producer: Mata Yamamoto, Tom Luddy

Screenplay: Paul Schrader, Leonard Schrader

Director: Paul Schrader

Photography: John Bailey

Music: Philip Glass

Editor: Michael Chandler

Production Design: Eiko Ishioka

Costumes: Etsuko Yagyu

Sound: Leslie Shatz

Cast: Ken Ogata (Yukio Mishima), Massayuki Shionoya (Morita), Hiroshi Mikami (Cadet), Junkichi Orimoto (General Mashita)

Return to Oz

Year of Release: 1985

Running Time: 110m

Production Company: Silver Screen Partners/Disney

Releasing Company: Buena Vista

Director: Walter Murch

NB: George Lucas simply received a "Special Thanks" credit at the end of the movie, along with his associate Robert Watts.

Latino

Release Date: 1986

Running Time: 105m

Production Company: Lucasfilm

Releasing Company: Cinecom

Executive Producer: George Lucas (uncredited)

Producer: Benjamin Berg

Screenplay: Haskell Wexler

Director: Haskell Wexler

Photography: Tom Sigel

Music: Diana Louie

Editor: Robert Dalva

Cast: Robert Beltran, Tony Plana, Annette Cardona, Ricardo Lopez, Louis Torrentes, Julio Medina, James Karen, Juan Carlos Ortiz

Labyrinth

Year of Release: 1986

Running Time: 100m

Production Company: Lucasfilm/Henson Associates

Releasing Company: Columbia Tri-Star

Executive Producer: George Lucas

Producer: Eric Rattray

Screenplay: Terry Jones

Story: Jim Henson, Dennis Less

Director: Jim Henson

Photography: Alex Thomson

Music: Trevor Jones, David Bowie (songs only)

Editor: John Grover

Production Design: Elliot Scott

Costumes: Brian Froud, Ellis Flyte

Special Effects: George Gibbs

Sound: Peter Sutton

2nd Unit Director/Photography: Peter MacDonald

3rd Unit Director/Photography: Jimmy Devis

Concept Design: Brian Froud

Cast: David Bowie (King of the Goblins), Jennifer Connelly (Sarah), Toby Froud (Toby)

Howard the Duck (aka Howard: A New Breed of Hero)

Year of Release: 1986

Running Time: 111m

Production Company: Lucasfilm

Releasing Company: Universal

Executive Producer: George Lucas

Producer: Gloria Katz, Robert Latham Brown

Screenplay: Willard Huyck, Gloria Katz

Comic Strip: Steve Gerber

Director: Willard Huyck

Photography: Richard H. Kline

Music: John Barry, Thomas Dolby (songs only)

Editor: Michael Chandler, Sidney Wolinsky

Production Design: Peter Jamison

Costumes: Joe Tompkins

Cast: Lea Thompson (Beverly Switzer), Jeffrey Jones (Doctor Jennings), Paul Guilfoyle (Lieutenant Welker), Tim Robbins (Phil Blumburtt), Liz Sagal (Ronette), Tommy Swerdlow (Ginger Moss), Richard Edson (Ritchie), Chip Zien (Howard's Voice)

Captain Eo

Year of Release: 1986

Running Time: 15m

Production Company: Lucasfilm/Disney

Releasing Company: Disney

Executive Producer: George Lucas

Producer: Rustly Lemorande

Screenplay: George Lucas

Director: Francis Ford Coppola

Photography: Vittorio Storaro

Music: Michael Jackson

Production Design: Geoffrey Kirkland, John Napier

Costumes: John Napier

Choreography: Jeffrey Hornaday

Cast: Michael Jackson (Captain Eo), Anjelica Houston (Evil Queen)

Powaqqatsi

Year of Release: 1988

Running Time: 97m

Production Company: Cannon/Golan-Globus

Releasing Company: Cannon

Director: Godfrey Reggio

NB: This was a George Lucas and Francis Ford Coppola "Presentation"

Willow

Year of Release: 1988

Running Time: 121m

Production Company: Lucasfilm/Imagine

Releasing Company: MGM-UA

Executive Producer: George Lucas

Producer: Nigel Wooll

Screenplay: Bob Dolman

Story: George Lucas

Director: Ron Howard

Photography: Adrian Biddle

Music: James Horner

Editor: Daniel Hanley, Michael Hall

Production Designer: Allan Cameron

Costumes: Barnara Lane

Special Effects: Dennis Muren, Michael Lantieri, John Richardson, Phil Tippettt

Sound: Ben Burtt, Ivan Sharrock, Gary Summers, Shawn Murphy

2nd Unit Director: Michael Moore

2nd Unit Photography: Paul Beeson

Stunt Co-ordinator: Gerry Crampton

Cast: Warwick Davis (Willow), Val Kilmer (Madmartigan), Joanne Whalley-Kilmer (Sorsha), Jean Marsh (Queen Bavmorda), Patricia Hayes (Raziel), Billy Barty (High Aldwin), Pat Roach (Kael), Gavin O'Herlihy (Airk),

The Land Before Time

Year of Release: 1988

Running Time: 70m

Production Company: Amblin/Sullivan-Bluth

Releasing Company: Universal

Executive Producer: George Lucas, Steven Spielberg, Frank Marshall, Kathleen Kennedy

Producer: Don Bluth, Gary Goldman, John Pomeroy

Screenplay: Stu Krieger

Story: Tony Geiss, Judy Freudberg

Director: Don Bluth

Music: James Horner

Production Design: Don Bluth

Editor: Dan Molina, John K. Carr

Voices: Pat Hingle, Helen Shaver, Candice Houston, Gabriel Damon, Judith Barsi, Will Ryan, Burker Barnes

Tucker: The Man and His Dreams

Year of Release: 1988

Running Time: 111m

Production Company: Lucasfilm/American Zoetrope

Releasing Company: Paramount

Executive Producer: George Lucas

Producer: Fred Roos, Fred Fuchs

Screenplay: Arnold Schulman, David Seidler

Director: Francis Ford Coppola

Photography: Vittorio Storaro

Music: Joe Jackson, Carmine Coppola

Editor: Priscilla Nedd

Production Design: Dean Tavoularis

Costumes: Milena Canonero

Special Effects: David Pier

Sound: Richard Beggs

Cast: Jeff Bridges (Preston Tucker), Joan Allen (Vera Tucker), Martin Landau (Abe Karatz), Frederic Forrest (Eddie Dean), Mako (Jimmy Sakuyama), Lloyd Bridges (Homer Feguson), Elias Koteas (Alex Tremulis), Christian Slater (Junior)

Indiana Jones and the Last Crusade

Year of Release: 1989

Running Time: 127m

Production Company: Lucasfilm

Releasing Company: Paramount

Executive Producer: George Lucas, Frank Marshall

Producer: Robert Watts

Screenplay: Jeffrey Boam

Director: Steven Spielberg

Photography: Douglas Slocombe

Music: John Williams

Editor: Michael Kahn

Production Design: Elliot Scott

Costumes: Anthony Powell, Joanna Johnston

Special Effects: Michael McAlister, George Gibbs

Sound: Ben Burtt, Richard Hyams

2nd Unit Director: Michael Moore, Frank Marshall

Additional Photography: Paul Beeson

Stunt Co-ordinator: Vic Armstrong

Cast: Harrison Ford (Indiana Jones), Sean Connery (Doctor Henry Jones), Denholm Elliott (Marcus Brody), Julian Glover (Walter Donovan), John Rhys-Davies (Sallah), Alison Doody (Doctor Elsa Schneider), River Phoenix (Young Indy), Michael Byrne (Vogel), Robert Eddison (Knight), Kevork Malikyan (Kazim), Michael Sheard (Hitler)

Radioland Murders

Year of Release: 1994

Running Time: 108m

Production Company: Lucasfilm

Releasing Company: Universal

Executive Producer: George Lucas

Producer: Fred Roos, Rick McCallum

Screenplay: Gloria Katz, Willard Huyck, Jeff Reno, Ron Osborn

Story: George Lucas

Director: Mel Smith

Photography: David Tattersall

Music: Joel McNeely

Editor: Paul Trejo

Production Design: Gavin Bocquet

Costumes: Peggy Farrell

Cast: Brian Benben (Roger), Ned Beatty (General Whalen), Michael McKean (Rick Rochester), Mary Stuart Masterson, Brion James, George Burns, Bobcat Goldthwaite, Christopher Lloyd, Scott Campbell, Corbin Bernsen, Michael Lerner, Stephen Tobolowsky, Larry Miller, Anita Morris, Robert Walden, Rosemary Clooney, Billy Barty, Bo Hopkins, Robert Klein, Harvey Korman, Peter MacNicol, Jack Sheldon

Star Wars Trilogy Special Edition *(Comprising Star Wars: Episode IV - A New Hope, Star Wars: Episode V - The Empire Strikes Back, Star Wars: Episode VI: Return of the Jedi)*

Release Date: 1997

Production Company: Lucasfilm

Releasing Company: Twentieth Century Fox

Executive Producer: George Lucas

Producer: Rick McCallum

Editor: Tom Christopher

Additional Special Effects: Dennis Muren, Bruce Nicholson, Alex Seiden, John Knoll, Dave Carson, Stephen Williams, Joseph Letteri, Tom Kennedy, Ned Gorman

Star Wars: Episode I - The Phantom Menace

Year of Release: 1999

Running Time: 135m

Production Company: Lucasfilm

Releasing Company: Twentieth Century Fox

Executive Producer: George Lucas

Producer: Rick McCallum

Screenplay: George Lucas

Director: George Lucas

Photography: David Tattersall

Music: John Williams

Editor: Paul Martin Smith

Production Design: Gavin Bocquet

Costumes: Trisha Biggar

Special Effects: John Knoll, Dennis Muren, Rob Coleman, Scott Squires

Sound: Ben Burtt

Make-up and Creature Effects: Nick Dudman

Stunt Co-ordinator: Nick Gillard

Concept Design: Doug Chiang

2nd Unit Director: Roger Christian

2nd Unit Photography: Giles Nutgen

Camera Operator: Trevor Coop

First Assistant Director: Chris Newman

Cast: Ewan McGregor (Obi-Wan Kenobi), Jake Lloyd (Anakin Skywalker), Natalie Portman (Queen Amidala), Liam Neeson (Qui-Gon Jinn), Anthony Daniels (C-3PO), Kenny Baker (R2-D2), Frank Oz (Yoda), Ian McDiarmid (Senator Palpatine), Warwick Davis (Wald), Terence Stamp (Supreme Chancellor Valorum), Hugh Quarshie (Captain Panaka), Brian Blessed (Boz Nass), Celia Imrie (Bravo Five), Adrian Dunbar (Bail Organa), Pernilla August (Shmi Skywalker), Samuel L. Jackson (Mace Windu), Ray Park (Darth Maul), Ahmed Best (Jar Jar Binks), Michaela Cottrell (Jedi Councilor), Ray Griffiths (Gonk), Friday Wilson (Handmaiden)

Appendix Three

Television Productions Made by Lucasfilm

The Ewok Adventure: Caravan of Courage

Year of Release: 1984

Running Time: 100m

Production Company: Lucasfilm/Korty Films

Broadcast Company: ABC

Executive Producer: George Lucas

Producer: Thomas G. Smith

Screenplay: Bob Carrau

Story: George Lucas

Director: John Korty

Photography: John Korty

Music: Peter Bernstein

Editor: John Nutt

Production Design: Joe Johnston

Costumes: Cathleen Edwards, Michael Becker

Special Effects: Michael Pangrazio

Sound: Randy Thom

Narrator: Burl Ives

Cast: Aubree Miller, Warwick Davis, Eric Walker, Fionnula Flanagan, Guy Boyd, Debbie Carrington, Dan Fishman

Ewoks: The Battle for Endor

Year of Release: 1985

Running Time: 100m

Production Company: Lucasfilm

Broadcast Company: ABC

Executive Producer: George Lucas

Producer: Thomas G. Smith

Screenplay: Jim Wheat, ken Wheat

Story: George Lucas

Photography: Isidore Mankofsky

Music: Peter Bernstein

Editor: Eric Jenkins

Production Design: Joe Johnston, Harley Jessup

Costumes: Michael Becker

Special Effects: Michael J. McAlister

Sound: Randy Thom

Cast: Aubree Miller, Warwick Davis, Wilford Brimley, Sian Phillips, Carel Struycken, Eric Walkler, Niki Bothelo

The Ewoks and Droids Adventure Hour

Year of Release: 1985

Running Time: 50m Episodes

Production Company: Lucasfilm/Nelvana

Broadcast Company: ABC

Executive Producer: Miki Herman

Music: Stewart Copeland, Taj Mahal (!)

Voices: Anthony Daniels, Cree Summer Francks, Jim Henshaw

The Great Heep

Year of Release: 1986

Running Time: 50m

Production Company: Lucasfilm/Nelvana

Broadcast Company: ABC

Exectutive Producer: Miki Herman

Screenplay: Ben Burtt

Director: Clive Smith

Music: Patricia Cullen, Patrick Gleeson, Stewart Copeland (songs), Derek Holt (songs)

Production Design: Joe Johnston

Sound: Ben Burtt

Voices: Anthony Daniels, Winston Rekert, Graeme Campbell, John Baldry

Ewoks

Year of Release: 1986

Running Time: 25m episodes

Production Company: Lucasfilm/Nelvana

Broadcast Company: ABC

Executive Producer: Elana Lesser, Cliff Ruby

Music: Patrick Gleeson

Voices: Sue Murphy, Jeanne Reynolds, James Cranna, Denny Delk

Maniac Mansion

Year of Release: 1990

Running Time: 25m episodes

Production Company: Lucasfilm/Atlantis Films/The Family Channel/YTV/Canada Inc.

Broadcast Company: The Family Channel

Exectuive Producer: Eugene Levy, Barry Jossen, Peter Sussman

Photography: Ray Braustein

Music: Louis Natale

Production Design: Stephen Roleff

Cast: Joe Flaherty, John Hemphill, Deb Faker, Cathleen Robertson, George Buza, Mary Charlotte Wilcox, Martin Short (guest)

The Young Indiana Jones Chronicles

Episode Titles: *My First Adventure, Passion For Life, The Perils of Cupid, Travels with Father, Journey of Radiance, Spring Break Adventure, Love's Sweet Song, Trenches of Hell, Demons of Deception, The Phantom Train of Doom, Oranga: The Giver and Taker of Life, Attack of the Hawkmen, Adventures in the Secret Service, Espionage Escapades, Tales of Innocence, Daredevils of the Desert, Mask of Evil, Treasure of the Peacock's Eye, Winds of Change, Mystery of the Blues, The Scandal of 1920, Hollywood Follies*

Year of Release: 1992

Running Time: 50m episodes

Production Company: Lucasfilm

Broadcast Company: ABC

Executive Producer: George Lucas

Producer: Rick McCallum

Screenplay: Carrie Fisher, Jonathan Hensleigh, Frank Darabont, Matthew Jacobs, Jonathan Hales, Ben Burtt, Gavin Scott, Reg Gadney, Rosemary Anne Sisson, Julie Selbo

Story: George Lucas

Director: Nicolas Roeg, Dick Maas, Mike Newell, Bille August, David Hare, Terry Jones, Gillies McKinnon, Jim O'Brien, Syd McCartney, Rene Manzor, Joe Johnston, Ben Burtt, Robert Young, Michael Schultz, Gavin Millar, Vic Armstrong, Deepa Mehta, Simon Wincer

Photography: David Tattersall, Jorgen Persson, Giles Nuttgens, David Higgs, Oliver Stapleton, Ashley Rowe, Miguel Icaza Solana

Music: Laurence Rosenthal, Joel McNeely

Editor: Ben Burt, Paul Martin Smith, Tom Christopher, Joan E. Chapman, Janus Billeskov-Jansen, Louise Ruback, Edgar Burcksen

Production Design: Gavin Bocquet, Ricky Eyres

Costumes: Trisha Biggar, Charlotte Holdich

Main Cast: Sean Patrick Flanery, Corey Carrier, Margaret Tyzack, George Hall, Lloyd Owen, Ruth DeSosa

Guest Stars: Jean-Pierre Aumont, Paul Freeman, Lukas Haas, George Corraface, Max Von Sydow, Michael Gough, Dorothy Tutin, Vanessa Redgrave, Kenneth Haig, Ian McDiarmid, Jacqueline Pearce, Maria Charles, Tom Bell, Freddie Jones, Ronald Fraser, Benedict Taylor, Christopher Lee, Jean-Pierre Cassel, Joss Ackland, Kenneth Cranham, Tim McInnerny, Timothy Spall, Harry Enfield, Terry Jones, William Hootkins, Liz Smith, Pernilla August, Catherine Zeta Jones, Peter Firth, Bob Peck, Adrian Edmondson, Tom Courtney, Cyril Cusack, Anna Massey, Michael Kitchen, Josef Sommer, Jerone Krabbe, Harrison Ford, Anne Heche

Appendix Four

Chronologigal list of films featuring ILM effects.
Those noted with an asterix denote an Academy Award for best special effects.
TVM denotes television movie.

Star Wars (1977) *

The Empire Strikes Back (1980) *

Raiders of the Lost Ark (1981) *

Dragonslayer (1981)

E.T. - The Extra Terrestrial (1982) *

The Dark Crystal (1982)

Poltergeist (1982)

Star Trek II: The Wrath of Khan (1982)

Twice Upon a Time (1982)

Return of the Jedi (1983) *

The Ewok Adventure: Caravan of Courage
  (1984 - TVM)

Indiana Jones and the Temple of Doom (1984) *

The Neverending Story (1984)

Starman (1984)

Star Trek III: The Search for Spock (1984)

Back to the Future (1985)

Amazing Stories (1985 - TV series)

Cocoon (1985) *

Enemy Mine (1985)

Ewoks: The Battle for Endor (1985 - TVM)

Explorers (1985)

Mishima (1985)

Out of Africa (1985)

The Goonies (1985)

Young Sherlock Holmes (1985 - aka *Young
  Sherlock Holmes and the Pyramid of Fear*)

The Golden Child (1986)

Howard the Duck (1986 - aka *Howard - A
  New Breed of Hero*)

Captain Eo (1986 - Disney theme park
  attraction)

Labyrinth (1986)

Star Trek IV: The Voyage Home (1986)

The Money Pit (1986)

Empire of the Sun (1987)

Harry and the Hendersons (1987 - aka *Bigfoot
  and the Hendersons*)

Batteries Not Included (1987)

Innerspace (1987) *

Star Tours (1987 - Disney theme park
  attraction)

*Star Trek: The Next Generation - Journey to
  Farpoint* (1987 - TVM)

The Witches of Eastwick (1987)

Caddyshack II (1988)

Cocoon: The Return (1988)

Who Framed Roger Rabbit? (1988) *

Star Trek (1988 - Universal theme park
  attraction)

Willow (1988)

The Last Temptation of Christ (1988)

Always (1989)

The Abyss (1989) *

Body Wars (1989 - Disney theme park
  attraction)

Back to the Future Part II (1989)

Tummy Trouble (1989 - short)

Skin Deep (1989)

Field of Dreams (1989)

The 'burbs (1989)

Ghostbusters II (1989)

Indiana Jones and the Last Crusade (1989)

Dreams (1990 - aka Akira Kurosawa's
Dreams)

Roller Coaster Rabbit (1989 - short)

Die Hard 2 (1990 - aka Die Hard 2: Die
Harder)

Ghost (1990)

The Godfather Part III (1990)

The Hunt for Red October (1990)

Joe vs the Volcano (1990)

Star Trek VI: The Undiscovered Country
(1991)

Backdraft (1991)

The Doors (1991)

Hook (1991)

The Rocketeer (1991)

Switch (1991)

Terminator 2: Judgement Day (1991) *

Hudson Hawk (1991)

Alive (1992)

The Young Indiana Jones Chronicle (1992 -
TV series)

Memoirs of An Invisible Man (1992)

Death Becomes Her (1992) *

Fire in the Sky (1993)

Jurassic Park (1993) *

Meteorman (1993)

Schindler's List (1993)

Rising Sun (1993)

The Nutcracker (1993)

Manhattan Murder Mystery (1993)

The Last Action Hero (1993)

Baby's Day Out (1994)

Maverick (1994)

The Hudsucker Proxy (1994)

The Mask (1994)

Radioland Murders (1994)

Disclosure (1994)

The Flintstones (1994)

Forrest Gump (1994) *

Star Trek: Generations (1994)

Wolf (1994)

Village of the Damned (1995)

Sabrina (1995)

Jumanji (1995)

The American President (1995)

Casper (1995)

The Indian in the Cupboard (1995)

Congo (1995)

In the Mouth of Madness (1995)

Daylight (1996)

Twister (1996)

Star Trek: First Contact (1996)

Eraser (1996)

101 Dalmatians (1996)

Dragonheart (1996)

Mars Attacks! (1996)

Mission: Impossible (1996)

The Lost World: Jurassic Park 2 (1997)

Men in Black (1997)

Spawn (1997)

Speed 2: Cruise Control (1997)

Flubber (1997)

The Star Wars Trilogy Special Editions (1997)

Star Trek: Insurrection (1998)

Deep Impact (1998)

Saving Private Ryan (1998)

Small Soldiers (1998)

Star Wars: Episode I - The Phantom Menace
(1999)

INDEX

References to photographs are followed by an asterisk